1–2 CORINTHIANS

WESLEY BIBLE STUDIES

wphonline.com

Copyright © 2014 by Wesleyan Publishing House
Published by Wesleyan Publishing House
Indianapolis, Indiana 46250
Printed in the United States of America
ISBN: 978-0-89827-884-2
ISBN (e-book): 978-0-89827-885-9

CONTENTS

INTRODUCTION

Meeting Challenges Head-On

With the eyes of the world glued to him, Nick Wallenda completed a nighttime tightrope walk across Niagara Falls on June 16, 2012. The event was extremely challenging, but Nick Wallenda met it head-on and succeeded.

On October 16, 2012, Felix Baumgartner jumped from a balloon more than 120,000 feet in the air—near the edge of space—and completed a record freefall. He met the astounding challenge head-on and succeeded.

After four unsuccessful attempts to swim 110 miles from Cuba to Florida, sixty-four-year-old Diana Nyad completed her dream on September 2, 2013, and she did so without a shark cage. The event was challenging, but Diana Nyad met it head-on and succeeded.

Challenges like those faced by Nick, Felix, and Diana are self-imposed, but most often challenges arise from circumstances that we didn't choose. Nevertheless, we can meet them head-on and successfully surmount them. As you study 1 and 2 Corinthians, you will see how the apostle Paul successfully addressed challenges posed by the church at Corinth. What you learn from Paul you can apply to similar challenges today.

THE CHALLENGE OF IMMATURITY

Although the believers at Corinth possessed many spiritual gifts, they failed to use them. Furthermore, they lacked spiritual wisdom, love, and unity. If they had been wise and loving, they would not have lined up behind their favorite leaders. They would have understood that Jesus is the church's only foundation. They would have recognized that each leader simply plays a divinely appointed role in building the church. Paul addressed each of the matters directly, definitively, and lovingly.

THE CHALLENGE OF BAD RELATIONSHIPS
Marriages, lawsuits, church discipline, and divisions about eating meat offered to idols needed apostolic attention, and Paul provided it. Likewise, relationships in churches today can be challenging, but this study of 1 and 2 Corinthians offers wise counsel.

THE CHALLENGE OF DOCTRINAL DEFICIENCY
The Corinthian believers had a poor understanding of spiritual gifts. They clamored for what they thought were the best ones, and they envied those who had gifts they wanted. Paul informed them that the Holy Spirit distributes spiritual gifts as He chooses and intends believers to use them to edify others.

The Corinthians needed to grasp the doctrine of the resurrection and realize its profound impact on their future, but also their present. A correct view of the resurrection would help them abound in the work of the Lord.

THE CHALLENGE OF CONFUSED WORSHIP
Worship in the Corinthian church was disorderly. Paul met this challenge by prescribing worship that was decent and orderly.

THE CHALLENGE OF SPREADING THE GOSPEL
Like almost any church, the church at Corinth needed to spread the good news. Paul explained that Satan had blinded the minds of the lost, but Paul offered strong motivation: God

changes minds and hearts. He can transform sinners into new creations, and He has commissioned Christians to serve as His ambassadors. However, as Paul pointed out, the treasure of the gospel is in clay vessels. We ought to be humble as we share this treasure with others.

THE CHALLENGE OF SUFFERING

Paul assured the Corinthians that suffering is only for a brief time and someday every Christian will have a brand-new body. He had suffered extreme hardship and pain to carry the gospel throughout the Roman Empire, but he delighted in all his afflictions and trials because Christ's power rested on him.

A rewarding study lies ahead, but you must be a diligent student of the Word. Accept the challenge!

THE CHURCH IS CALLED TO BE HOLY

1 Corinthians 1:1–10; 3:10–17

God is developing a holy people.

Does a Christian meat butcher display holiness if he presses his thumb onto the scale when he weighs a pound of sliced roast beef? Does an auto dealer portray holiness if he knowingly sells a defective car to an unsuspecting buyer? Will a family gain a clear concept of holiness if their Christian neighbors yell and scream at each other? How holy will a community think a church is if that church experiences a series of splits?

This study introduces us to the church at Corinth, a church that needed to be holy in a very unholy city.

COMMENTARY

The city of Corinth in the time of Paul was the stereotypical sailor's port, with every corruption imaginable. Ships would unload in Corinth, and their goods would be transported by wagon (smaller ships would be dragged on rollers) to the northern side of the isthmus. Today, there is a canal across, begun by the Romans and finished in the nineteenth century. There were at least twelve pagan temples. The most infamous was dedicated to Aphrodite, the goddess of love, whose resident temple prostitutes would converge on the city each evening. Sex with a temple prostitute put funds into the temple and was considered an act of worship. Corinth's reputation for perversion was so widely known that when the Romans would show a Corinthian onstage, he was always drunk. In Greek "to Corinthianize" was a verb meaning "to practice sexual perversion."

Corinth needed the gospel—not only because of the corrupt environment, but because the gospel could spread from there to every urban area of commercial importance. But the atmosphere was not conducive to church planting. Paul's relationship with the Corinthian church was stormy from the beginning. It appears Paul wrote at least four letters to Corinth. Besides 1 and 2 Corinthians there were two letters called the "previous letter" (1 Cor. 5:9–11) and the "sorrowful letter" (2 Cor. 2:4; 7:8–9) that have been lost.

The picture of the Corinthian church is not pretty. Paul sent emissaries (Timothy—1 Cor. 4:17; and Titus—2 Cor. 2:12–13; 7:6–16) to try to get the church on track. Apollos refused to go (1 Cor. 16:12). Paul went to Corinth a number of times and not always with good results (2 Cor. 10:10–11; 13:1–2). There were divisions in the church (1 Cor. 1:11), personal attacks against Paul (1 Cor. 2:1–10), immorality (1 Cor. 5:1), and even the Lord's Supper was perverted (1 Cor. 11:20–22). They were arrogant (1 Cor. 5:2). Perhaps if they compared themselves to the corruption of their city they might have some spiritual pride, but if they used the measure of other churches they should have been humbled.

Set Apart and Called to Be Holy (1 Cor. 1:1–3)

Paul, called to be an apostle (v. 1) tells us more than who wrote the letter. It tells us Paul believed he was sent by God as a messenger for Jesus Christ. The term **apostle** is one Christians appropriated from the Jews, who called their official envoys from Jerusalem to the Hellenistic world *apostles*. Paul saw himself as an official envoy of Jesus Christ sent directly **by the will of God** (v. 1).

Whatever the problems in Corinth, Paul addressed the believers there as **the church of God in Corinth** (v. 2). Paul declared them **sanctified in Christ Jesus** (v. 2). It is clear from 1 Corinthians 3:1–3 that Paul did not think much of their spiritual maturity, so what was he saying? The Greek term **sanctified** (1:2) has two meanings. The first is to be "separate from common condition and use; dedicated" (*The Analytical Lexicon to the Greek New Testament*, p. 50). William Barclay said the root meaning of holy is *different*. In this sense, the church of Corinth was sanctified. They were separated from the common in Corinth, they were saved, and they had an initial point of spiritual beginning. Without that, Paul could not have written to them as he did. There were those in the Corinthian church who wanted to be different, separate, and dedicated to the Lord. They were, without doubt, God's church in Corinth.

WORDS FROM WESLEY
1 Corinthians 1:1

Paul, called to be *an apostle*—There is great propriety in every clause of the salutation, particularly in this, as there were some in the church of Corinth, who called the authority of his mission in question, *through the will of God*—Called the commandment of God, 1 Tim. 1:1. This was to the churches the ground of His authority; to Paul himself, of a humble and ready mind. By the mention of God, the authority of man is excluded, (Gal. 1:1) by the mention of the will of God, the merit of Paul [is excluded], (ch. 15:8, &c.) (ENNT)

But beyond this, they were **called to be holy** (v. 2). The second aspect of sanctification is purity or cleansing: "to make clean or holy in the ethical sense, though the idea of consecration is not necessarily lacking" (*Beacon Dictionary of Theology*, p. 470). This is the aspect of sanctification missing in the Corinthian experience. In 1 Corinthians 3:1, Paul said, "Brothers, I could not address you as spiritual." While recognizing their place within the church, he also recognized their lack of spiritual maturity. They were separated, but neither pure nor mature.

The Corinthian measuring stick was their corrupt society and themselves, not **all those everywhere who call on the name of our Lord Jesus Christ—their Lord and ours** (1:2). There is a fine line between contextualizing the gospel in a society and mixing pagan practice with Christian practice. One way to keep the vision clear is to look at the church in general and ask how we measure up to the whole. The Corinthians came up short. They were separated but not pure by any standard beyond their own society. God has a higher standard.

Grace and peace to you from God our Father and the Lord Jesus Christ (v. 3) is a distinct Christian greeting with the addition of **grace** and **the Lord Jesus Christ** to a standard Jewish greeting. The concept of grace is fundamental to understanding scriptural revelation. While **grace** may be defined as unmerited favor from God, it is favor to which one must respond. While grace may be identified in its various aspects (for example, prevenient grace, saving grace, sanctifying grace, etc.), there is only one grace. God's grace offered before salvation is the same grace offered after salvation to lead and guide and give spiritual growth. A positive response to grace is faith; a negative response to grace is sin; but some response is required.

Peace (*shalom*) is the sign of the kingdom of God. Abraham and his descendants had been looking for a kingdom that would give them security and thus peace. They had thought it would be in a walled city or an established dynasty like David's or Solomon's. After exile, they thought it would come with return to the land. The Maccabeans thought it would come through the overthrow of foreign oppression. Peace either never came or never lasted. Jesus made it clear that the kingdom and real peace is within His people (John 14:27; Luke 17:21).

The Lord Jesus Christ (1 Cor. 1:3) is a name configuration. **Lord** has it roots in the Old Testament, the name for God, YHWH, as it was used by the Jews. **Jesus** is indicative of His humanity,

God with us to save us. **Christ** calls on all the prophecies and authority accorded to the Messiah. Verse 3 is a New Testament Christian greeting loaded to overflowing with faith and doctrine.

Spiritual Gifts Do Not Indicate Spiritual Maturity (1 Cor. 1:4–10)

In dealing with spiritual pride, it is important to understand **grace given you** (v. 4), being **enriched in every way—in all your speaking and in all your knowledge** (v. 5), and the fact that **you do not lack any spiritual gift** (v. 7). This is not contingent on who you happen to be. Nor is it contingent on your mighty, personal, spiritual presence. It is contingent on being **in Christ Jesus. For in him you have been enriched** (vv. 4–5). It is Jesus who **will keep you strong** (v. 8). It is **God, who has called you** and who is also **faithful** (v. 9).

WORDS FROM WESLEY

1 Corinthians 1:9

"But how then is God faithful?" I answer, in fulfilling every promise which he hath made, to all to whom it is made, all who fulfill the condition of that promise. More particularly, (1) "God is faithful" in that "he will not suffer you to be tempted above that you are able to bear" (1 Cor. 10:13). (2) "The Lord is faithful, to establish and keep you from evil" (if you put your trust in Him); from all the evil which you might otherwise suffer, through "unreasonable and wicked men" (2 Thess. 3:2–3). (3) "Quench not the Spirit; hold fast that which is good; abstain from all appearance of evil; and your whole spirit, soul, and body shall be preserved blameless unto the coming of our Lord Jesus Christ. Faithful is he that calleth you, who also will do it" (1 Thess. 5:19, &c). (4) Be not disobedient unto the heavenly calling; and "God is faithful, by whom ye were called, to confirm you unto the end, that ye may be blameless in the day of our Lord Jesus Christ" (1 Cor. 1:8–9). Yet, notwithstanding all this, unless you fulfill the condition, you cannot attain the promise.

"Nay, but are not 'all the promises, yea and amen?'" They are firm as the pillars of heaven. Perform the condition, and the promise is sure. Believe, and thou shalt be saved. (WJW, vol. 10, 290)

In verse 7, **therefore** points back to the **testimony about Christ** that **was confirmed in you** (v. 6). Because you have been saved, the spiritual gifts you need are available to you. Spiritual gifts are not dependent on spiritual maturity (3:1–3) but rather on salvation by faith in Christ. This is profound. Spiritual gifts may be enhanced as the individual grows in faith and maturity, but God gives these gifts early in our salvation experience. These spiritual gifts may be indicators that an individual is "sanctified in Christ Jesus" (1:2 — set apart, saved, initial sanctification), but they are not an indicator that the individual is filled with the Spirit, in sense of being entirely sanctified, or mature. The signs of entire sanctification are purity and maturity. The Corinthians had spiritual gifts without maturity.

The Corinthian church had misunderstood the gifts as being measurements of spiritual depth and maturity. This brought **divisions** (v. 10) and disunity. They had begun to follow individual giftedness (vv. 12–17) as measurements of spiritual depth, rather than being blessed by others' spiritual gifts and in turn blessing others with their spiritual gifts.

Sanctified Builders Build Rather Than Boast (1 Cor. 3:10–17)

Paul began this section with a testimony: **By the grace God has given me** (v. 10). If grace requires a response, the best way to spiritual maturity would not be by the "amount" of the grace given, but by the response that follows. Paul's illustration was of building material given by God. God gave Paul foundation material, so he said, **I laid a foundation as an expert builder, and someone else is building on it** (v. 10). The foundation was the mystery of Christ (Eph. 3:1–6) and the extension of the covenant beyond the ethnic family of Abraham, even to the Gentile Corinthians. Others were by grace given different building materials, but the foundation, **Jesus Christ** (1 Cor. 3:11), cannot be changed, no matter what the building materials. God gives grace, but men and women must respond to it with cooperative works. Some only build with the most elemental building materials: **wood, hay or straw** (v. 12). Others build with elements that will last: **gold, silver, costly stones** (v. 12). The grace God gives is not for the recipients to compare volume and beauty of building materials but to build the church (1 Cor. 12:12–28).

WORDS FROM WESLEY

1 Corinthians 3:11

"Salvation by faith only ought not to be preached as the first doctrine, or, at least, not to be preached to all." But what saith the Holy Ghost? "Other foundation can no man lay than that which is laid, even Jesus Christ." So then, that "whosoever believeth on him shall be saved," is, and must be, the foundation of all our preaching; that is, must be preached first. "Well, but not to all." To whom, then, are we not to preach it? Whom shall we except? The poor? Nay; they have a peculiar right to have the gospel preached unto them. The unlearned? No. God hath revealed these things unto unlearned and ignorant men from the beginning. The young? By no means. "Suffer these," in anywise, to come unto Christ, "and forbid them not." The sinners? Least of all. "He came not to call the righteous, but sinners to repentance." Why then, if any, we are to except the rich, the learned, the reputable, the moral men. And, it is true, they too often except themselves from hearing; yet we must speak the words of our Lord. For thus the tenor of our commission runs, "Go and preach the gospel to every creature." If any man wrest it, or any part of it, to his destruction, he must bear his own burden. But still, "as the Lord liveth, whatsoever the Lord saith unto us, that we will speak." (WJW, vol. 5, 14)

There is another cooperative element to this building illustration: Some settle for the less-substantial over the substantial. Perhaps carrying stone is harder work than bundling straw. Gold is a greater responsibility than wood. Why take the chance? The goal is not to be busy, but to build substantially. **His work will be shown for what it is . . . the fire will test the quality of each**

man's work (3:13). Where would we be today if Paul had not built a solid, substantial foundation?

Finally, Paul reminded us this was more personal than it seemed. It is not just "the church" we are building. **God's temple is sacred, and you are that temple** (v. 17). Our response to grace affects others (the church) but it affects us, too. Some are building a thatched hut rather than a golden temple. In Christ, we are sanctified (set apart) and called to be holy, the furthest possible point spiritually from where we began and the closest possible point to what God wants us to be, nearest to himself. He gives grace but expects us to build with substance.

WORDS FROM WESLEY

1 Corinthians 3:17

If any man destroy the temple of God—Destroy a real Christian, by schisms, or doctrines fundamentally wrong, *him shall God destroy*—He shall not be saved at all; not even as through the fire. (ENNT)

DISCUSSION

What should the church be known for? Some might argue that it should be known for the best potlucks in the county. Others might want it to be known for its charitable outreach. A few might insist it should be known for its great music. The church *should* be known for its holiness.

1. Do you see any similarities between Corinthian culture and modern culture? Defend your answer.

2. Do you see any similarities between the Corinthian church and some churches today? Defend your answer.

3. Paul was called to be an apostle. Why do you agree or disagree that no one should become a pastor without being called by God to the position?

4. Read 1 Corinthians 1:2–3. How do you think holy people differ in lifestyle from the general population?

5. Why do you agree or disagree it is significant that "grace" precedes "peace" in Paul's greeting?

6. How is it possible for an immature believer to possess several spiritual gifts?

7. How does it encourage you today to know that God is faithful?

8. What do you think is more important: a church's physical size or its spiritual depth? Why?

9. How can you build well in preparation for the inspection Paul mentioned in 1 Corinthians 3:12–15?

10. How can you help others build well?

PRAYER

Lord, thank You for the grace You have given us through Jesus Christ. Through that grace, please help us choose holiness each day this week.

THE CHURCH IS BUILT ON GOD'S WISDOM

1 Corinthians 2:1–16; 3:1–3

God's wisdom is greater than all worldly wisdom.

A church may rise like a rocket but fall like a rock if it is not built of God's wisdom. Human wisdom, charisma, wealth, and the presence of celebrity personalities cannot create the kind of church that passes the test of time and God's thorough inspection. To be great in God's eyes, a church must rest on the firm foundation of Jesus and rely on divine wisdom.

In His wisdom, God planned our salvation. He based it on the crucifixion of His Son. Human wisdom might have planned something far different, but only the cross bridges the gulf that separates sin and a holy God. True wisdom values the cross and builds a holy life on the finished work of Jesus.

COMMENTARY

Nowhere was Paul more transparent than in this passage. Were it not for what he revealed about himself here, we would likely misjudge both his temperament and his personality.

In his other Epistles and especially in Acts, Paul's demeanor might be considered hard-nosed, with a zealousness that left little room for anyone who hesitated in the faith (see his "one strike" policy in Acts 15:37–38). His Pharisaism was redeemed, to be sure, but he still seems to have retained some of that demanding forcefulness he had prior to conversion.

But here suddenly—almost embarrassingly—he showed his inner sense of vulnerability. Through this divinely inspired writing, we see this strongest of New Testament believers share touching aspects of his life that give comfort to those of us who aren't so strong.

Not only was there an identification with weaker believers—a good hope in itself—but in this moment of openness, Paul revealed the bedrock of his life that brings powerful godly wisdom and authority for even the most timid of believers. Their lives (and ours) can have the same confidence and courage Paul demonstrated.

Paul's Unique Authority—What It Wasn't (1 Cor. 2:1–4)

Much biblical teaching involves some form of contrast—for example, the Proverbs and many of Jesus' teachings, such as His wisdom on good deeds, prayer, and fasting in Matthew 6. Here Paul used contrast too, stating both what did and did not give him authority and wisdom to convince and convict people of truth.

Neither **eloquence** (v. 1) nor **persuasive words** (v. 4) mattered to Paul. He belittled his ability to speak, perhaps hearkening back to Moses and his thrice-repeated excuse as to why he shouldn't lead the people (Ex. 4:10; 6:12, 30). In an ironic wonder, this letter records the most eloquent love composition ever written (1 Cor. 13). Yet, there as well as here, he struck down eloquence as the basis upon which one would have authority or wisdom.

What a needed lesson. When we are swayed by eloquent politicians or a sales pitch, may we learn deeply and absolutely that eloquence is *not* the criteria for making a wise decision. Paul hit that first and hardest: His message, authority, and wisdom did not come from eloquence. **I resolved to know nothing** (2:2). Second, Paul spoke to the singleness of his mission by stating what he resolved not to do. That word **resolved** is important, because we know Paul was, in fact, knowledgeable about many things. He was a tentmaker by training (Acts 18:3). He knew the Hebrew Bible (Old Testament) with all its nuances and implications. He knew a good deal about political science and Roman and Jewish jurisprudence. He was a seasoned traveler. All these would have made him a wise authority across a broad spectrum. Yet Paul did not use any of that as the basis for his wisdom. Whatever he had of worldly knowledge or experience meant nothing. That is, all the things we would rely on to demonstrate our great wisdom and authority, Paul vetoed. Much like he did when he wrote to the Philippian church about another set of criteria—such as a first-class pedigree, education, and moral life (Phil. 3:4–7)—none of these things meant anything *in comparison to* knowing Christ personally.

Consider the implications of his "know nothing except ____" focus. Think, for example, of the TV shows where to win you must know trivia facts. In our information-overloaded world, without ever leaving your computer, you could spend a lifetime becoming an expert in whatever you chose to study. All too often we confuse knowledge with wisdom.

Paul's assertion that what we all strive for is worth nothing in comparison to knowing Christ must have raised eyebrows, both for original recipients and for many today. But the real surprise is 1 Corinthians 2:3: **I came to you in weakness and fear, and with much trembling.** What must they have thought when they read this? The one who came across so forcefully here revealed another side.

Fear, or *phobos*, is where we get the English word *phobia*. When was the bold apostle Paul afraid? **Trembling**? Legs shaking and knees knocking? Who would have thought? There was no arrogance or stubborn, demanding authority here.

Paul may have been referring to something more profound than a human trait. This fear was the fear of the Lord. That phrase cannot be separated, defined in detail, and then combined to get the meaning. It is a biblical concept used over a hundred times—most pointedly in Psalm 111:10 and Proverbs 9:10, where it says "The fear of the LORD is the beginning of wisdom." At first thought, this fear of the Lord is a foreign concept in our democratic world, but perhaps it is akin to the first time you hold a newborn baby. For many, that happens with fear and trembling; we think they might break.

Maybe not exactly the same, but Paul's fear was that he would not faithfully and clearly present Jesus. His fear was that people would not take seriously the message. His fear was that somehow he might bring reproach on God and God's Son, Jesus.

WORDS FROM WESLEY

1 Corinthians 2:3

Q. But does he not disclaim any such assurance [of salvation] in those words, "I was with you in weakness, and in fear, and in much trembling" (1 Cor. 2:3)?

A. By no means. For these words do not imply any fear either of death or hell. They express only a deep sense of his utter insufficiency for the great work wherein he was engaged. (WJW, vol. 8, 292)

Paul's Unique Authority and Wisdom—What It Was (1 Cor. 2:2, 4–5)

This stance led to what Paul identified as the basis of his authority and what made him wise. Simply this: knowing Jesus Christ and God's Spirit of power.

Jesus Christ . . . crucified (v. 2) was the only subject that interested Paul. His resolve was to minimize worldly wisdom and maximize godly wisdom. The only true relevance of knowing anything else was to show how much superior Jesus is to any human achievements or power or wisdom, certainly to include religious knowledge, which corresponded with his letter to the

Philippian church (Phil. 3:13). That is a consistent theme of all the apostles and church leaders: Peter on the day of Pentecost (Acts 2:16ff.), Steven (Acts 6), and Philip (Acts 8:35), to name a few. Jesus, crucified and risen, was the ultimate in wisdom and knowledge (Col. 2:3). The more time spent with Him, the wiser one would become.

In our world there are so many plans, seminars, diets, programs, and books on how to get ahead, how to be wiser than others. More pointedly, there is an overabundance of religious programs and experts and books. As good as any of that may be, Paul said it is in knowing Jesus all the way through to crucifixion (and resurrection, though not stated in this verse) that one gains wisdom. Anything else is only valued to the degree it helps one know Jesus.

Spirit's power . . . God's power (1 Cor. 2:4–5). Here is where Paul obtained his authority and supernatural wisdom: the Holy Spirit of God working in him. By comparison, all of what we ordinarily think of as most important is trumped by something virtually no one considers important.

If there is any doubt about this, consider the "power brokers" our culture counts as wise: mass media, university professors, movie stars, producers, superstar athletes. How many times will a recognized movie personality give an opinion on national policy, and it is trumpeted as if it were the most astute observation? How often does a network anchor speak a few sentences and have them taken for absolute truth?

Paul wrote to dispel that tendency; his argument and plea was that even though the world does not see or accept God's power or wisdom, surely the Corinthian believers would see and make choices accordingly—choices to be obedient and responsive to the Spirit of God, who gives power and wisdom over that of the world.

Who Can and Cannot Receive and Understand This Wisdom (1 Cor. 2:6–16)

Paul's theme throughout the book so far is that there are two opposing, mutually exclusive definitions of wisdom. While not spending time on defining the wisdom of the world, he did make the distinction that draws a line between human wisdom and godly wisdom: what one does with Jesus. For those who reject Him, everything godly remains a secret (or mystery). For those who accept Jesus, the secrets of God are revealed.

All people start on equal footing and are presented with two possibilities: accepting or rejecting Jesus. At this point, the roads divide, going down their respective paths of worldly wisdom or godly wisdom, to where life becomes more muddled or more clear, and the effects of that initial choice are magnified. One path will come **to nothing** (v. 6). The other path will open to understanding and a glory beyond anything our earthly imagination could conceive (v. 9). Surely Paul was thinking of such passages as Proverbs 4:18–19 and the teachings of Jesus in the Sermon on the Mount (Matt. 6:13–14), where He spoke of two roads to travel.

WORDS FROM WESLEY
1 Corinthians 2:6

Yet we speak wisdom—Yea, the truest and most excellent wisdom, *among the perfect*—Adult, experienced Christians. By wisdom here he seems to mean, not the whole Christian doctrine, but the most sublime and abstruse parts of it. *But not the wisdom* admired and taught by the men *of this world, nor of the rulers of this world,* Jewish or Heathen, *that come to nought*—Both they and their wisdom, and the world itself. (ENNT)

Paul quoted from Isaiah (64:4; 65:17) but went back to creation (1 Cor. 2:9). The master plan from the beginning culminates in the life of Jesus. Because Jesus lived in historical time, Old Testament believers (through God-opened imaginations and accepting the promises) had to live with some mystery. To them, it was **God's secret wisdom** (v. 7). Even so, these old saints rejoiced in their limited understanding, as Jesus exclaimed in John 8:56. All the more condemnation accrues to present-day doubters who don't realize there is such wisdom. It was obvious to Paul that they had no inkling, otherwise they would not have crucified Jesus.

But now believers everywhere can know and experience the fullness of the life of Jesus Christ, as God's Spirit reveals to us, lives in us, and fills us with this Holy Spirit. Paul was almost bursting with this incredible news. No one in the history of the world had known this, but now it was here for the taking.

WORDS FROM WESLEY

1 Corinthians 2:12

"There is therefore now no condemnation to" these. There is no condemnation to them from God; for He hath *justified* them "freely by his grace, through the redemption that is in Jesus." He hath forgiven all their iniquities, and blotted out all their sins. And there is no condemnation to them from within; for they "have received not the spirit of the world, but the Spirit which is of God; that they might know the things which are freely given to them of God" (1 Cor. 2:12); which Spirit "beareth witness with their spirits, that they are the children of God." (WJW, vol. 5, 87)

In 1 Corinthians 2:14–16, Paul paused to summarize his letter so far. The person *without* God's Spirit does not and cannot understand spiritual truth; it is all foolishness. The person *with* God's Spirit at work within is able to judge accurately what is real and good in the world. Again he quoted from Isaiah (40:13). Go there and sit in God's counsel, where the heights of wisdom soar beyond human comprehension.

Baby Steps versus Mature Steps (1 Cor. 3:1–3)

To this point, Paul contrasted men's wisdom versus those with godly wisdom. Next he drew the difference between those who are "mature" (2:6) and those who are **mere infants** (3:1) This power and wisdom that no previous generation had access to should have been working in the lives of the believers—power beyond anything they had ever known; "deep things of God" (2:10) now opened up. And all "freely given" (v. 12).

WORDS FROM WESLEY
1 Corinthians 3:2

I fed you as babes *with milk*; the first and plainest truths of the gospel, So should every preacher suit his doctrine to his hearers. (ENNT)

But not much of that was happening in Corinth because they were acting like babies. Sometimes biblical illustrations are hard to get, but not this one; virtually no word study or commentary is necessary. While Paul later gave specific instances of their infant-like immaturity, we close this study with this final tragedy: that their lives were diminished by their choice not to claim the wisdom and power the Holy Spirit offered to them. The challenge is not only for a first-century individual and church, it is ours as well.

DISCUSSION

What does it take to build a great church? Would a church become great if it obtained a pastor with a string of post-graduate degrees or a gift of several million dollars? While neither of these unlikely possibilities is wrong, a church cannot be great unless it is built on the wisdom of God.

1. Why is human wisdom, no matter how extensive, inadequate for the preaching of the gospel?

2. Why is human wisdom, no matter how extensive, inadequate for the building of God's church?

3. Read 1 Corinthians 2:2–5. What personal characteristics do you discern about Paul in these verses?

4. Why do you agree or disagree that modern culture would like to get rid of the message of the cross?

5. What popular messages do you think some churches are substituting for the message of the cross? Explain your answer.

6. What value do you think there is for an unbeliever to read the Bible?

7. How does the Holy Spirit help you understand God's Word?

8. Read 1 Corinthians 3:1–3. In light of this passage, how would you define *worldliness*?

PRAYER

God, help us honor You as the source of our wisdom this week. Please empower us with Your Spirit to focus on Jesus today.

3

YOUR BODY—GOD'S TEMPLE

1 Corinthians 6:12—7:5

Honor God with your body.

No one who cares about his or her body rummages in garbage cans for daily meals (if it can be avoided). The thought of doing so is grotesque. But how often do some believers feast the eyes and sexual appetites on filthy movies, immoral TV shows, lewd Internet images, or racy magazines? Let's face it; such practices make about as much sense as trying to find nutritious food in garbage cans.

Does it matter what we feed our minds and bodies? This study points out that the believer's body is God's temple. The Holy Spirit resides in it. We are responsible, therefore, to keep the body pure.

COMMENTARY

In this first letter we have from Paul to the church at Corinth, we read the apostle's warning about the consequences of sexual immorality and his answers to questions about what is appropriate for Christians.

Your Body Belongs to God (1 Cor. 6:12–14, 19–20)

The topics of this section are your body, to whom it belongs, and how you should treat it. Paul wrote **that your body is a temple of the Holy Spirit, who is in you** (v. 19).

When people plan to live somewhere temporarily, they often rent rather than buying living space. Others rent because they cannot afford to buy, have no down payment, or think the selling price is too high. But none of these is true of God. **You are not your own; you were bought at a price** (vv. 19–20). The Holy Spirit intends to make your body His permanent dwelling. Since God owns everything, the price is not beyond His reach. In fact, the price has been paid at Calvary.

WORDS FROM WESLEY

1 Corinthians 6:20

Glorify God with your body and your spirit—Yield your bodies and all their members, as well as your souls and all their faculties, as instruments of righteousness to God. Devote and employ all ye have, and all ye are, entirely, unreservedly, and for ever to His glory. (ENNT)

Therefore honor God with your body (v. 20). Sometimes Christians ask whether they should participate in a certain activity, eat certain foods, or attend certain events. Some Christians resist the idea that they shouldn't do certain things they want to do. They are concerned about permissibility, rather than how to honor God with their bodies. Common questions include, "Can a Christian do this?" or "Will I go to heaven if I do this?" The apostle Paul addressed these kinds of issues with the Corinthian church. Perhaps his admonitions can help us as we wrestle with some of the same issues today.

Paul instructed us to think about the consequences of our choices. **"Everything is permissible for me"—but not everything is beneficial** (v. 12). People who wish to honor God with their bodies will consider the benefit or harm any given activity will have on their bodies. Rest, nutrition, and exercise should be maintained in careful balance for the benefit of physical health. Another factor Paul pointed out is control. **"Everything is permissible for me"—but I will not be mastered by anything**

(v. 12). Nothing you put into your mind or body should control you. Some experiences such as gambling, pornography, power, entertainment, and pleasure can become addictive. Some chemicals such as narcotics, tobacco, caffeine, and alcohol can take control of your mind and body. The question is not permissibility but control. Since your body is a temple of the Holy Spirit, and God is its owner, He should have control of His residence.

WORDS FROM WESLEY

1 Corinthians 6:12

All things, which are lawful for you, *are lawful for me: but all things are not always expedient*—Particularly when any thing would offend my weak brother; or when it would enslave my own soul. For though *all things are lawful for me, yet I will not be brought under the power of any*—So as to be uneasy when I abstain from it. For if so, then I am under the power of it. (ENNT)

Eternity is also to be considered when endeavoring to honor God with your body. In relation to food and the stomach, we are reminded that **God will destroy them both** (v. 13). Many people do not want to think about eternity, but Paul said you must consider eternity if you wish to honor God with your body. You will live differently if you realize you are in this world temporarily, but eternity is forever. In this world, many spend much of their time, money, and effort on things that will not last. Those who honor God with their bodies will focus on what lasts forever.

To rephrase Paul's admonition, you are not meant for immorality, but for immortality. **The body is not meant for sexual immorality, but for the Lord, and the Lord for the body** (v. 13). Sexual desires are part of our humanity, but we are not to simply act on our impulses and desires. Again, we are made **for the Lord** (v. 13). Satisfaction of sexual impulses lasts for a brief time, but **by his power God raised the Lord from the dead, and he will raise us also** (v. 14), indicating our eternal relationship with Jesus Christ.

Purity Provides Protection (1 Cor. 6:15–18)

Paul offered further insight into his earlier statement, "The body is not meant for sexual immorality" (6:13). Moral purity is often viewed—by both Christians and non-Christians—as a list of narrow rules and regulations. Here Paul provided reasons that moral purity is beneficial. He showed how sexual purity protects us spiritually, emotionally, and physically.

Not only did Paul describe our bodies as "a temple of the Holy Spirit, who is in you" (v. 19), but he reminded us our **bodies are members of Christ himself** (v. 15). His pointed question is, **Shall I then take the members of Christ and unite them with a prostitute?** (v. 15). One of the reasons Christians should be sexually pure is that sexual morality affects our spiritual relationship with Christ. As Christian believers, we cannot participate in sexual immorality without bringing Jesus into our actions. Again, Paul said, **he who unites himself with the Lord is one with him in spirit** (v. 17). Sexual purity protects you spiritually, and sexual immorality damages your spiritual relationship with Christ. One reason to stay morally pure is because you care about your spiritual relationship with Jesus Christ.

A second area of protection moral purity provides is emotional. Paul spoke of a oneness that is part of sexual intimacy. Even if sexual participation is purchased or casual, the principles that are part of our nature cannot be denied. When engaging in sexual intimacy, we are reminded that **the two will become one flesh** (v. 16). No matter the intention of the partners, when you engage in sexual intimacy, you give a part of yourself to the other person and receive part of that person to yourself. This oneness has an emotional component. You cannot buy protection for your heart or take a pill to heal the emotional effects of sexual immorality. Sexual immorality leaves you emotionally injured, hardened, or both. Purity provides emotional protection.

Perhaps the most obvious protection provided by moral purity is physical. Our culture is familiar with the acronyms STD (Sexually Transmitted Diseases), HIV (Human Immunodeficiency Virus), and AIDS (Acquired Immune Deficiency Syndrome). Added to these diseases is the risk of unwanted pregnancy. Even without modern science and medicine, it was obvious to Paul that sexual immorality is sin against our bodies. He stated that **he who sins sexually sins against his own body** (v. 18).

In light of the protection moral purity provides, Paul's admonition may seem obvious. **Flee from sexual immorality** (v. 18). Moral purity is not a code of narrow rules and regulations, but rather our creator God's provision of spiritual, emotional, and physical protection. The magnitude of human suffering that has been experienced by ignoring Paul's admonition is immeasurable.

The Sanctity of Intimacy in Marriage (1 Cor. 7:1–5)

Paul next turned his attention to answering a question that may have been posed by the Corinthians. It may be that his observations about the body and sexual immorality were preparing us for his answers in this section. While the question itself is not given, it is apparent that it dealt with whether Christians should marry or remain single.

Singles have sometimes been made to feel less than fulfilled, like second-class citizens. They may be questioned about when they will marry or if they have found someone. They may even be tagged with unflattering nicknames. But Paul's initial response to the Corinthians' question was an affirmation of singleness. **It is good for a man not to marry** (v. 1). He repeated his affirmation in verse 8 and identified personally with those who were unmarried.

WORDS FROM WESLEY

1 Corinthians 7:1

It is good for a man—Who is master of himself, not to touch a woman—That is, not to marry. So great and many are the advantages of a single life. (ENNT)

Without minimizing singleness, Paul also recognized marriage as God's sanctified relationship for sexual intimacy. To avoid sexual immorality **each man should have his own wife, and each woman her own husband** (v. 2). While Paul and other New Testament writers emphasized the community aspects of the church, notice that marriage is not to be communal. This simple statement is clear in its implications. One man is paired with one woman and vice versa in marriage. Monogamous, heterosexual marriage is God's chosen and only sanctified place for sexual relationships.

Paul took it a step further than this. He instructed husbands and wives to **fulfill** their **marital duty** (v. 3) to each other. Sex in marriage is not dirty or defiled. It is God's blessed and holy gift to a husband and wife. Humans did not create sex; God did. Genesis 1:27 states that God created them male and female. In Genesis 2, a more detailed account of this is given. "The LORD God made a woman . . . and he brought her to the man" (Gen. 2:22). The description continues with reference to uniting, becoming one flesh, and their nakedness. As noted above, "the two will become one flesh" (1 Cor. 6:16) is associated with the sexual relationship.

Continuing with this thought, Paul stated that **the wife's body does not belong to her alone but also to her husband. In the same way, the husband's body does not belong to him alone, but also to his wife** (7:4). Sexual immorality involves sexual

activity with someone whose body does not belong to you. Sexual
activity in marriage is blessed of God, because through exchang-
ing of wedding vows, you and your spouse have given your bodies
to each other and to none other. The marriage relationship is a
safe, holy place to practice God's gift of sexuality.

WORDS FROM WESLEY

1 Corinthians 7:4

The Holy Ghost says, "Marriage is honourable in all, and the
bed undefiled." Nor can it be doubted but persons may be as holy
in a married as in a single state.

In the latter clause of the sentence, the apostle seems to guard
against a mistake, into which some sincere Christians have fallen;
particularly when they have just found such a liberty of spirit as
they had not before experienced. They imagine a defilement
where there is none, "and fear where no fear is." And it is possible
this very fear of sin may betray them into sin. For it may induce
persons to defraud each other, forgetting the express determination
of the apostle: "The wife hath not power of her own body, but the
husband; and the husband hath not power of his own body, but
the wife" (1 Cor. 7:4). (WJW, vol. 11, 457)

To married couples the command is given: **Do not deprive
each other except by mutual consent and for a time, so that
you may devote yourselves to prayer** (v. 5). The basis of this
discourse about the sanctity of intimacy in marriage is based on
the earlier statement: **since there is so much immorality** (v. 2).
Sexual intimacy is not only allowed in marriage, it is mandated
as a means of avoiding sexual immorality.

Paul reminded us we have an enemy, **Satan**, who will try to
tempt you because of your lack of self-control (v. 5). The apostle
Peter cautioned us to be self-controlled and alert because our
enemy the Devil prowls around like a roaring lion looking for
someone to devour (1 Pet. 5:8). Jesus warned that "the thief

comes only to steal and kill and destroy" (John 10:10). Satan wants to destroy your marriage and steal your family from you. He will use every tool available for that purpose.

Satan has saturated our society with sexual stimulation. Much of the advertising and entertainment we see appeals to sexual appetites. Books, magazines, billboards, TV programs, commercials, computer images, and messages appeal to sexual impulses. We are drawn to laugh at, applaud, or accept the immoral. Satan bombards us with sexual images, endeavoring to raise unreasonable expectations and dissatisfaction in marriage relationships.

Along with sexual saturation, Satan keeps people so busy that little time is left for family relationships. This adds stress, tension, and fatigue to the other pressures of a family. While society is sexually oriented, many Christian couples are left deprived of appropriate intimacy. This leaves many susceptible to attraction to a person who is not their spouse. Satan uses an abundance of sexual messages to stimulate temptation, then wears down resistance through busyness, stress, and fatigue.

Paul called on Christian couples to be aware of Satan's tactics. We must be intentional in maintaining strong relationships with our spouses, including intimacy, to protect ourselves from temptation to sexual immorality. Many who have fallen into Satan's trap never expected it would happen to them and their marriage. As purity protects you spiritually, emotionally, and physically, intimacy with your spouse safeguards you from sexual immorality.

DISCUSSION

Should a Christian take care of his or her body? After all, isn't the spirit more important? Paul's teaching about God's temple should settle these questions conclusively.

1. Read John 14:16. Why do you agree or disagree that the Holy Spirit plans to dwell in every believer permanently?

2. According to 1 Corinthians 6:12, what principle should govern our moral choices? Do you think this principle applies to what we choose to eat? Why or why not?

3. How do you decide whether you should or should not do something like drink or smoke?

4. How can thinking about eternity strengthen your resolve to live for God?

5. Why do you agree or disagree that immorality is more blatant now than at any previous time?

6. How might Christian parents guard their children from harmful images shown on the movie screen, on TV, and through the Internet?

7. In what ways does illicit sexual behavior affect the marriage relationship?

8. Do you agree or disagree that contemporary culture's decline into sexuality immorality is beyond hope?

PRAYER

Creator God, You have fearfully and wonderfully made us. Let us treat these temples that are our bodies with respect for the handiwork You have invested in.

4

BOUND BY LOVE

1 Corinthians 8:1–13

Freedom with responsibility is love in action.

Sergio and Anna occasionally had a glass of wine with their dinner. One weekend, they made plans to eat with a new couple they had been getting to know at church. Because they knew Tim and Jennifer had both struggled with alcoholism before they met Christ, Sergio and Anna chose to refrain from displaying or consuming alcohol while their guests were in their home. Were Sergio and Anna being hypocritical or deceitful? No. They were simply choosing to love their brother and sister in Christ by behaving in a way that wouldn't tempt or cause the younger believers to engage in a practice they saw as sinful.

This study examines the role of love in our choices.

COMMENTARY

The apostle Paul experienced the city of Corinth on his second missionary journey in A.D. 51. With the help of Aquila and Priscilla, he planted a vibrant, growing church (Acts 18:1–18). But being a mature Christian in Corinth proved to be a challenge. The world the Christians were saved out of, and the culture they found themselves in, led to a number of questions about how to live the Christian life.

Corinth, a port city, was a center of trade and commerce for the ancient world. It attracted many vices. Corinthians were known for their drunkenness. Sexual promiscuity, including incest, was part of the culture. Worship of Aphrodite, the goddess of love, involved participating in sexual acts with temple prostitutes as well as sacrificing animals. People came from all over the then-known world to worship Aphrodite. Corinth also paid homage to the Greek god of the sea, Poseidon. The Corinthian economy relied on the sea. It was important to them that this god was appeased. Again, the way to appease a god was through animal sacrifice. The temple of Apollo was also located in Corinth. Apollo was the god of prophecy and agriculture and the protector of young men and women. Agriculture was important in this society. Again, the way to appease Apollo was through animal sacrifice.

Meat is an obvious byproduct of animal sacrifice. After a portion was given to the gods and a portion was taken by temple priests, the rest was taken to the city's meat markets. This created a moral dilemma for some in the church. The question was, "Is it right to eat meat that has been sacrificed to idols?"

The church sent word to the apostle Paul, asking him a number of questions. First Corinthians was written, in part, as a response to those questions. We can tell when Paul was responding to a question from Corinthians because the sections that answer a question begin, "Now about" (1 Cor. 7:1; 8:1; 12:1).

The Overriding Principle of Love (1 Cor. 8:1–3)

Some people thought it was alright to eat this meat. Others said, "I know what goes on in those temples; I worshiped there before I became a Christian. It is wrong to eat that meat."

Paul said, "You are asking a secondary question. The primary question is about how best to love your brothers and sisters in the faith." Paul argued that even if you have right thinking, deeper insight, and better logic than your brothers and sisters, you can still be wrong. **Knowledge puffs up, but love builds up** (v. 1). One can be right and still be wrong.

Many people have the need to be right and the need to be seen to be right. They spend a lot of time studying and learning so they can be right. Being right and being seen to be right puffs up their ego. Being a Christian, however, is not about building up your ego; it is about building up members of the body of Christ. Spiritually mature people, while they may have deeper insight and broader knowledge, know that loving the people around them is more important than correcting error. Spiritually mature people are humble about their knowledge (v. 2). Mature believers ask, "What does it mean to love God when I have more knowledge than my brothers and sisters?" They know that to use knowledge in a harmful way not only sins against the people in the church, but it sins against Christ (v. 12).

WORDS FROM WESLEY

1 Corinthians 8:2

If any man think he knoweth any thing—Aright, unless so far as he is taught by God, *he knoweth nothing yet as he ought to know*—Seeing there is no true knowledge without divine love. (ENNT)

Idols and the Modern World (1 Cor. 8:4–7)

So then, about eating food sacrificed to idols (v. 4). North American churches don't often encounter questions about meat sacrificed to idols. This does not mean the question is irrelevant. The same dynamic is replayed over and over in the modern church.

People who were saved from North American "pagan culture" often have weak consciences from the world they were saved out of. **Some people are still so accustomed to idols that when they eat such food they think of it as having been sacrificed to an idol, and since their conscience is weak, it is defiled** (v. 7). When these people participate in anything relating to that world, their conscience is defiled. What is more difficult for these people is seeing mature Christians participating in things from the world they were saved out of.

Some who were saved out of "sex, drugs, and rock and roll" hear music that emulates what they heard in the world and ask, "How can you be a Christian and listen to that?" Every time they hear that music, it takes them back to the time when they were living in sin. Some who were saved out of a gambling background ask, "How can you be a Christian and play cards?" Some who were saved out of alcoholism ask, "How can you be a Christian and drink?" Some who were saved out of a family in conflict ask, "How can we be a church and experience conflict?" When Paul addressed the question about meat sacrificed to idols, he dealt with all these questions and many more like them.

Paul wrote that **an idol is nothing at all** (v. 4). He was not saying this in the sense that there is nothing to these idols. In fact, he suggested there may be more to these gods than stone and metal (v. 5). He clarified in 10:19–20: "Do I mean then that a sacrifice offered to an idol is anything, or that an idol is anything? No, but the sacrifices of pagans are offered to demons, not to God."

WORDS FROM WESLEY

1 Corinthians 8:5

As there is but one God to us, though "there are gods many, and lords many" (1 Cor. 8:5); so to us there is but "one Mediator," or Intercessor, though we should grant there are many intercessors and mediators. For though the angels and saints may intercede for us in heaven, that no more makes them such intercessors as we may pray to, than because there are gods many, we may pray to them, as we do to the true God.

The Scripture knows no difference between a Mediator of intercession and redemption: He alone makes intercession for us that died and rose, and is at the right hand of God. And He alone has a right to our prayers, and to Him alone may we address them. (WJW, vol. 10, 105)

He was saying the power behind these idols is demonic. But Paul still said **an idol is nothing at all** (8:4) because **for us there is but one God, the Father, from whom all things came and for whom we live** (v. 6). An idol is nothing compared to the greatness of God. Your city may believe Poseidon is lord of the sea, but **there is but one Lord, Jesus Christ, through whom all things came and through whom we live** (v. 6). God the Father is the true God; compared to Him, all the gods and all the demons of hell are nothing. Jesus Christ is the true Lord of all, and compared to Him, all other lords are pretenders.

Spiritually mature people understand this. But this is a hard concept for those who have experienced the demonic power of the idols (v. 7). Many supernatural things, attributed to the gods, happened in Corinth. It was hard to have so much faith in God as to say, "That was nothing." But spiritually mature believers understood this was precisely the case.

WORDS FROM WESLEY
1 Corinthians 8:6

Yet to us Christians *there is but one God*—This is exclusive, not of the one Lord, as if He were an inferior Deity; but only of the idols, to which the one God is opposed: *from whom are all things*—By creation, providence and grace; *and we for him*—The end of all we are, have, and do: *and one Lord*—Equally the object of divine worship: *by whom are all things*—Created, sustained, and governed; *and we by him*—Have access to the Father and all spiritual blessings. (ENNT)

Doing What Is Right Can Be Wrong (1 Cor. 8:8–12)

The food offered to idols was not transformed in the offering. Even though this meat was used in the worship of demons, the meat itself was not contaminated. Paul said, **We are no worse**

if we do not eat, and no better if we do (v. 8). In other words, eating meat sacrificed to idols is amoral. It does not affect one spiritually. It is the same as eating any other meal. At least, that is the case for the spiritually mature. The spiritually mature understand who God is, who they are in Christ, and that the demonic can't touch them while they are in Christ. The spiritually immature, however, don't understand this.

There is a principle being alluded to in this passage that is stated in Romans 14:23: "But the man who has doubts is condemned if he eats, because his eating is not from faith; and everything that does not come from faith is sin." Even if a particular action is not wrong, if a person thinks it is wrong, for that person it is wrong. Something not intrinsically sinful is sinful to a person who believes what they are doing is not right. Part of living by faith is believing in the rightness of what they are doing. If anyone has doubts about how he or she is living, living in that way is sin.

That is why sacrificed food, while not wrong in itself, can defile a person with a weak conscience (1 Cor. 8:7). That defilement can lead to the destruction of that person's spiritual life (v. 11). Something that is not wrong in itself can destroy a person's soul. If a person facilitates that destruction, he or she is held accountable for that, even if what was done is not technically wrong (v. 12).

WORDS FROM WESLEY

1 Corinthians 8:11

And through thy knowledge shall the weak brother perish, for whom Christ died—And for whom thou wilt not lose a meal's meat, so far from dying for him! We see Christ died even for them that perish. (ENNT)

Living Well in Community (1 Cor. 8:13)

The most important consideration is not if an action is right or wrong, but how it affects the community. Paul was addressing how to live in community with those who are weak in conscience. He was not addressing how to live in community with those who are easily offended. People who come from legalistic backgrounds are offended by something that does not fit their brand of legalism. That is not what Paul was talking about. He was talking about those who have a weak conscience who would be led into doing something they were convinced was not right. Paul was trying to balance the idea of our freedom in Christ (v. 9) with our obligation to those who are weak in faith. His conclusion was that love trumps personal freedom.

His argument went like this: Those who are spiritually mature, because they have more knowledge (v. 7) and a stronger conscience, are people of influence. How they behave influences those who are weak in faith. A person with a strong faith can eat meat offered to idols with a clear conscience. However, if a people with weak consciences see a mature person eating this meat, they may think, "If that person is mature in the faith can eat this meat, I can too" (v. 10). But as they eat the meat, all the associations of idol worship come back to them, and they can't help but feel what they are doing is wrong. They are not eating by faith; they are eating under the influence of others. Their conscience is defiled. When people live contrary to their conscience, they are on the road to destruction.

Paul argued the spiritually mature are not sinning by eating meat sacrificed to idols; they are sinning because they are wounding the conscience of a weaker brother or sister. This is not only a sin against the person of weaker conscience; this is a sin against Christ (v. 12). The weakest Christian is still a part of the body of Christ. Whenever we sin against him, we are sinning against Christ.

Paul's response to this dynamic is **if what I eat causes my brother to fall into sin, I will never eat meat again** (v. 13). Our actions need to be tied more to loving God and loving others than what we see as right.

North American culture is obsessed with rights. Non-Christian culture says, "I have the right to what I want to do as long as I don't hurt anyone." Christian culture says, "I have the right to do what I want to do as long as what I am doing is right." The Bible, however, takes a different view: The gospel values freedom, but the gospel values love more than freedom. We are called to live in such a way as not to be a stumbling block to our brothers and sisters. If exercising our rights will lead others to go against their conscience, we are called to deny ourselves those rights.

DISCUSSION

There are two ways to look at our freedom in Christ. One way is to say, "I am free to engage in that activity, and if a weaker Christian gets offended, tough!" The other way is to say, "I am free to engage in that activity, but I will not do so because I do not want to be a stumbling block to a weaker Christian." Reflect on which attitude honors the Lord and which attitude you tend to have.

1. Why would it have been difficult to become a mature Christian in Corinth?

2. Why do you agree or disagree that it is hard to maintain high moral standards when you are surrounded by pagans?

3. In what situation(s) might a believer be right but still be wrong?

4. In what kinds of activities might a knowledgeable believer engage that might offend a weaker believer?

5. How prevalent is idol worship in your community? Defend your answer.

6. How would you respond if a church member tried to start a football pool among the other members? Why would you feel that way?

7. Define a "weak conscience."

8. Do you agree or disagree that, in the final analysis, a Christian does not have any personal rights?

PRAYER

Lord, let us conduct ourselves in ways that are sensitive to the needs of others and honoring to You always.

5

OUR FOUNDATION IS FIRM

1 Corinthians 10:1–17

God enables us to stand firm in the faith.

Garden of the Gods in Colorado Springs is a popular tourist attraction. Its red rock formations rise high into the clear blue sky and offer scenic settings for both amateur and professional photographers. The rocks attract not only photographers, but also climbers, most of whom come prepared with climbing equipment. Others, however, come equipped only with an unfounded sense of self-confidence. The self-confidence often results in some climbers becoming trapped high on narrow ledges from which firefighters must rescue them. Sometimes, a climber falls and suffers severe injury or even death.

This study helps us avoid a spiritual fall.

COMMENTARY

Luke related the story of the beginning of the church at Corinth in Acts 18. Paul's ministry in the city began by meeting in the Jewish synagogue and soon moved next door to the home of a fellow believer, Titius Justus. Other early believers in Corinth included Aquila, Priscilla, and Crispus. While some early converts were Jews, they were soon joined by Greeks and other Gentiles.

The diversity of the church included not only Jews and non-Jews, but persons of wealth and the poor, men and women, Greek slaves and Roman freedmen, saints and sinners. The variety of backgrounds in these church participants contributed to some of the difficulties and divisions that plagued the church; however, their common love for Jesus Christ bound them in unity.

Since the religious root of many Corinthian Christians was Judaism, it is possible some members of the church practiced *both* Judaism and Christianity. It is likely their Jewish religious roots inclined them to return to the Judaism with which they were familiar. These are the persons to whom Paul appealed in chapter 10 with his reference to the Old Testament. At the end of chapter 9, Paul used an illustration from Grecian games to capture the attention of Greek Christians, which further affirms his audience.

Gnosticism, which originated in the Greek word for *knowledge*, challenged the Corinthian church, as well as most other early churches. Among its characteristics was the pursuit of knowledge for the sake of knowledge itself, marking its adherents with intellectual superiority. This pride and overconfidence was not different from the insidious challenges arising in the Corinthian church, or within those Israelites who had followed Moses into the desert.

The context in 1 Corinthians 8–10 relates to idolatry, and the "indulge[nce] in pagan revelry" (10:7) that characterized idol worship. These patterns of behavior enticed the Corinthians and challenged their newfound Christianity.

Israel's Wandering in the Desert (1 Cor. 10:1–6)

Paul's Jewish readers were well aware of perhaps the greatest work of God in their Old Testament history. They could not plead to being **ignorant**, but these incidents stretch far beyond solely the **forefathers** (v. 1) of the Jews, and reach to the entirety of the human race.

Our **forefathers** and their extended families received special protection by the visible symbol of God's abiding presence. **The cloud** (v. 1) of God provided relief from the desert heat and protection from the enemy. In perhaps the most miraculous of situations, **they**

all passed through the sea (v. 1). The greatest story of God's working in Israel's history enabled the Israelites to cross the Red Sea on dry land and enveloped the Egyptians in its tumultuous waters. Moses' significant guidance as a great respected leader of the nation of Israel led to him being a mediator for the nation with their God. Moses was the one who initiated the people of God into God's covenant. His profession of faith in God became their profession of faith. The identification with Moses was intense to the point that it could be said **they were all baptized into Moses** (v. 2).

This is a type of what was to come, for Christians are to identify with Jesus Christ in their baptism. Moses, in the reality of the exodus event and the freeing of the Israelites from Egyptian slavery, also represents Christ, who leads those who will follow out of bondage to sin. Just as Moses baptized into a life of freedom, so are persons who follow Christ baptized into His life of freedom.

At the root of this close identification with Moses was the rock. Paul explained, **that rock was Christ** (v. 4). From this living rock emitted **the same spiritual food and . . . drink** (vv. 3–4) that was shared by all. The breadth should be noted here—the commonality among the diverse believers in the church at Corinth is shared with the church of the ages. All of us drink from the rock of Christ, who provides **spiritual food** and **spiritual drink**.

The **spiritual food and . . . drink** that sustained the Israelites in the desert were the heavenly manna and water from a dry rock. These were supernaturally provided to satisfy the hunger and thirst of God's people. But more than mere physical sustenance, these were examples of God's salvation and continued protection for His people. The imperfect verb tense of **drank** in verse 4 shows continued action throughout their journey. The Israelites continued to drink **from the spiritual rock . . . and that rock was Christ** (v. 4). God's supernatural abiding presence demonstrated by the manna and water **occurred as examples** (v. 6) and provided a foretaste of the body and blood of Jesus Christ celebrated in the Lord's Supper (10:16).

But despite God's continued blessing of food and drink to His people, their consistent disobedience meant **God was not pleased with most of them** (v. 5). Their refusal to follow God's ways resulted in death outside the Promised Land, and **their bodies were scattered over the desert** (v. 5). Only Joshua and Caleb were spared.

WORDS FROM WESLEY

1 Corinthians 10:4

And all drank the same spiritual drink (typical [symbolic] of Christ, and of that cup which we drink). *For they drank out of the spiritual* or mysterious rock, the wonderful streams of which followed them in their several journeyings, for many years, through the wilderness. And that rock was a manifest type [symbol] of Christ, the rock of eternity, from whom His people derive those streams of blessings, which follow them through all this wilderness. (ENNT)

The (Bad) Example of Idolatry (1 Cor. 10:6–12)

Now these things occurred as examples to keep us from setting our hearts on evil things as they did (v. 6). The continued disobedience of the Israelites resulted in their deaths. We should learn from their errors and avoid repeating their actions. They brought judgment upon themselves through their disobedience as they were caught up in idolatry (v. 7). So satisfied were they with the practice of **evil things** (v. 6) that they **sat down to eat and drink and got up to indulge in pagan revelry** (v. 7).

The **pagan revelry** that accompanied idol worship was not foreign to the Corinthians. Not unlike the pagan practices that went on in Corinth, the ancient Israelites had constructed an idol in the form of a calf—Apis, the bull-god of Egyptian fertility—

when Moses seemed delayed upon the mountain in Exodus 32. Upon his return from Mount Sinai, Moses found them indulging in revelry (Ex. 32:6). In similar fashion, the men of Israel indulged in **sexual immorality** (1 Cor. 10:8) with the Moabite women in Numbers 25 after joining them in the worship of Baal of Peor. The action led to the death of **twenty-three thousand of them** (1 Cor. 10:8). Yet Israel continued to **test the Lord** with their appetite for evil things so the Lord sent **snakes**, which **killed** many (v. 9). But still they grumbled **and were killed by the destroying angel** (v. 10).

WORDS FROM WESLEY

1 Corinthians 10:6

Now these things were our examples—Showing what we are to expect, if enjoying the like benefits, we commit the like sins. (ENNT)

These are lessons **written down as warnings for us** (v. 11). They are not merely old stories or history without meaning. These are for those **on whom the fulfillment of the ages has come** (v. 11), persons who now see God and His work more clearly than ever before because of the example of Jesus Christ, God's very Son (Heb. 1:1–2).

These examples are warnings. Our sense of self-sufficiency must not overtake the necessity for us to **be careful that** we **don't fall** (1 Cor. 10:12). Temptation lurks around the corner to deceive and to undermine if we **think** we **are standing** (v. 12). The security we have in personal strength, accompanied by a refusal to accept God's help, can rapidly lead to a fall.

Victory Over Temptation (1 Cor. 10:13)

Temptation . . . is common to humanity (v. 13). Temptation is not unique in the human experience, but it is proportioned to human strength, as the origin of this Greek word **common** indicates. Temptation is not in this sense supernatural, beyond that with which humanity can cope with God's help. Christians today continue to experience the distraction of evil, just as humanity has been plagued since the fall in the garden of Eden. Today's temptations are no more unusual than those that confronted saints of old or even Jesus Christ.

God does not promise that temptation can be avoided. But He has promised that He **is faithful** and will not abandon us in temptation. Nor will He **let** us **be tempted beyond what** we **can bear** (v. 13). Times of temptation are occasions for a faith workout. They serve as an exercise program to strengthen spiritual muscles and commitment to Jesus Christ. Human muscle must be exercised to be at its best; and so spiritual life is strengthened when temptation is resisted.

WORDS FROM WESLEY

1 Corinthians 10:13

Let us begin with the observation which ushers in this comfortable promise: "There hath no temptation taken you but such as is common to man." Our translators seem to have been sensible that this expression, *common to man*, does by no means reach the force of the original word. . . . I believe the sense of it can only be expressed by some such circumlocution as this: "Such as is suited to the nature and circumstances of man; such as every man may reasonably expect, if he considers the nature of his body and his soul, and his situation in the present world." If we duly consider these, we shall not be surprised at any temptation that hath befallen us; seeing it is no other than such a creature, in such a situation, has all reason to expect. (WJW, vol. 6, 477)

Temptation provides continued opportunity for the exercise of the human will. The power of temptation cannot compel us to turn to sin. **God is faithful** and a way of standing **up under it** or **a way out** will be provided (v. 13). Often it is not an easy escape, but the provision for added strength and increased spiritual maturity will enable a more ready escape or stronger stand in the next temptation. God promises not exemption from trials, but His presence and sustenance in the hour of those trials.

The Unity of the Lord's Supper (1 Cor. 10:14–17)

Therefore—because of the distinct example we have of God's continued provision for His people and because of His promise to strengthen us to stand up in the hour of temptation—**flee from idolatry** (v. 14). Idolatry is the center of sin today, just as in the time of Moses. Idolatry places something at the center of life other than God. It may be time, money, power, or a host of other things; but it always places our selfish desires before God's.

This was no gentle admonition, but a command to flee with all our might, the only reasonable alternative for **sensible people** (v. 15). Rather than exercising his apostolic authority, Paul appealed to his readers' rational thinking. The price of idolatry is seen in the example of the Israelites. The faithfulness of God is evident. Now, what viable alternative is there?

Jesus provides a sustaining reminder of God's presence in the Lord's Supper. The **cup of thanksgiving** (v. 16) reminds us of the **blood of Christ** shed on the cross. The **bread that we break** reminds us of the **body of Christ** (v. 16) bruised for our iniquity. Participation as **we all partake** (v. 17) reminds us of the intensity of the relationship God desires and intends for His children.

We, who are many, are one body (v. 17) in Christ "whether Jews or Greeks, slave or free" (12:13). We **all partake of the one loaf** (10:17). There is no inequality at the table of our Lord. There is no head or foot, no first or second chair, no recognition of better and best—but a common participation in one body and one loaf. The Lord's Table draws the diverse community of Christ together like no other sacred event. It affirms our oneness in Christ regardless of ethnicity, race, gender, economic status, denomination, or spiritual idiosyncrasies. As **we, who are many, affirm that we are one body** (v. 17) in our Savior Jesus Christ, we are enabled to stand firm in the faith at all times.

WORDS FROM WESLEY

1 Corinthians 10:16

This is also an ordinary, stated means of receiving the grace of God, is evident from those words of the apostle, which occur in the preceding chapter: "The cup of blessing which we bless, is it not the communion," or *communication*, "of the blood of Christ? The bread which we break, is it not the communion of the body of Christ" (1 Cor. 10:16)? Is not the eating of that bread, and the drinking of that cup, the outward, visible means, whereby God conveys into our souls all that spiritual grace, that righteousness, and peace, and joy in the Holy Ghost, which were purchased by the body of Christ once broken and the blood of Christ once shed for us? Let all, therefore, who truly desire the grace of God, eat of that bread, and drink of that cup. (WJW, vol. 5, 195)

DISCUSSION

We have all gasped upon seeing images of houses disappear into sinkholes. Their destruction was swift because they did not have a firm foundation. Reflect on how firm your foundation is when Satan tries to use temptation to sink you.

1. Why would Judaism fail to provide a firm foundation for the Corinthian believers?

2. How would Gnosticism pose a challenge to the Corinthians' faith?

3. Why do you agree or disagree that the wide diversity of people and backgrounds in the Corinthian church challenged the believers' faith?

4. Read 1 Corinthians 10:1–3. How did God take care of His people when they wandered in the desert?

5. What personal lessons can you apply from the examples given in verses 6–10?

6. Did you ever stumble or fall spiritually when you thought such a thing could not happen? What were the circumstances?

7. How does the rock in the desert (v. 4) picture Christ?

8. How does Communion picture Christian unity?

9. Why do Christians need one another?

PRAYER

Lord, thank You for giving us options to withstand temptation. Please give us the wisdom to know when we're facing temptation, and the strength to choose against it.

6

AN INVITATION TO SUNDAY DINNER

1 Corinthians 11:17–34

Places at the table of the Lord are reserved not for
the worthy, but for the redeemed.

Has this happened to you? You left the house, got into your car, but suddenly realized you forgot your car keys. And then, to your dismay, you couldn't remember where you left them. Did you leave them in the coat you wore yesterday? Did you drop them in a drawer? Maybe you can blame the forgetfulness on the hippocampus, a region of the brain involved in the formation and retrieval of memories. It often deteriorates with age.

We all forget things occasionally, but we must never forget that Jesus shed His blood for our sins. As this study shows, the Lord's Supper helps us remember our Lord's death.

COMMENTARY

In this portion of Scripture, Paul had to address the impropriety he encountered with the Corinthian church in their dishonoring the Lord's Supper. In a matter of years, a sacred remembrance of our Lord had become nothing more than an opportunity to get together for a feast and grow divisions within the body. While there is nothing wrong with a fellowship meal, it was clear to Paul that the attitudes and behavior of the Corinthian church had gone to the extreme and were cultivating sin within the church. This included their manner of taking Communion.

Benjamin Franklin once said, "Poverty wants some things, Luxury many things, and Avarice all things." The sin was not in the meal itself but the behavior of those who had much and refused to share. Maybe avarice was a sin of the Corinthian church.

Paul's understanding of the Lord's Supper came from others who had received the message directly from Christ. He wanted the church to understand the difference between the paschal setting of the Lord's Supper and the covenantal setting, as explained in the Synoptic Gospels. John the Baptist called Christ the "true Lamb of God" (John 1:29), foretelling that Christ's bruised body and spilled blood would be offered for the redemption of those who accept Christ as Savior. Paul affirmed that Christ *is* our Passover, or paschal (Greek *pascha*) offering (1 Cor. 5:7). This is the divine fulfillment of the redemption covenant. Christ gave ratification of the covenant meal by celebrating it with His disciples before His death. In the upper room, Christ used bread and wine as symbols for the new covenant He was establishing. The bread and wine were to be used in remembrance of His sacrificial death, and celebrated within the fellowship of Christian believers. It also anticipates the banquet to be celebrated at the second coming.

The Lord's Supper is a reenactment of Christ's sacrifice on the cross. The sacrifice itself is not repeated. What happens is a remembrance, a reassurance of the covenant promise God made to His people. Paul was stressing that the elements the Corinthian church was partaking in were a means of grace, and the Holy Spirit was present for their spiritual nourishment.

These lessons are the same for the present and future church. Today, whether we refer to the sacrament as commemorative, memorial, covenant, Communion, Eucharist, or Lord's Supper, some things are assured. Christ is present with believers by the Holy Spirit; so Christ is the Host at the table. He is our spiritual sustenance. We have fellowship with Him and one another.

The class system of rich and poor seems to be one underlying theme of dissension. The rich were bringing plenty of food, but sharing it only with others of their class. Many poor had nothing and remained hungry. This had become a source of humiliation to the poor. While Paul acknowledged that human nature makes us all vulnerable to division, such division leads to unholy behavior.

Each person should test his or her own heart, examine, to be sure he or she is aware of the significance and act of communing with God, and a spiritual means to grace.

WORDS FROM WESLEY

1 Corinthians 11:18

"When ye come together in the church," the Christian congregation, "I hear that there are divisions" (the original word here also is . . . *schisms*) "among you." But what were these schisms? The apostle immediately tells you (v. 20): "When you come together," professing your design is "to eat of the Lord's Supper, every one of you taketh before another his own supper," as if it were a common meal. What then was the schism? It seems, in doing this, they divided into little parties, which cherished anger and resentment one against another, even at that solemn season. (WJW, vol. 6, 403)

Divisions and Differences (1 Cor. 11:17–22)

Paul first addressed the divisions. He indicated that he didn't believe everything he heard, but knew there must be some basis (vv. 17–18). In verse 19, when he wrote **differences among you to show which of you have God's approval**, Paul noted that divisions help distinguish the faithful. The agape meal preceded the Communion service. Paul expressed disapproval of the mockery the Corinthian church was making of the Lord's Supper. They were abusing the agape love feast that accompanied the Supper. The rich were eating to the point of gluttony, while others went hungry. The same was due to drinking wine and becoming drunk. He also indicated that there was a lack of order in the manner in which the meal was served (v. 21). Paul summed up his disgust with their behavior by accusing them of despising **the church of**

God and humiliating **those who** had **nothing** (v. 22) to share. There is a lesson here for today's church to be mindful of the needs of others and to maintain order in our church functions, particularly in partaking of the Lord's Supper.

Communing through the Lord's Supper (1 Cor. 11:23–26)

In looking at the references to the manner in which our Lord initiated the sacrament of Communion in this passage (see chart below), Christ gave thanks, in the true Jewish tradition, and became our Eucharist—which means *thanksgiving*—as He gave the symbol of broken bread to represent His body (vv. 23–24). In the same way, He blessed the cup as a representation of His blood that would be shed. Just as Jews celebrated Passover as a commemorative feast, the disciples were called to share a memorial meal, even though they did not understand the full meaning at the time. This commemorates the spiritual bond that unites all Christians to Christ's death.

WHAT	Partake of bread and cup	1 Corinthians 11:24–25
WHEN	Whenever you partake	1 Corinthians 11:25
WHY	In remembrance of Christ's sacrifice, as a proclamation until He returns	1 Corinthians 11:26

Paul admonished the believers not to come in so hungry that they would become guilty of gluttony. They should eat at home before coming, so that the purpose of the feast was not lost. Paul's reference to eating could be used for either the agape meal or the Lord's Supper. Jesus said to His disciples, "I have eagerly desired to eat this Passover with you before I suffer" (Luke 22:15). Christ, knowing what was to come, was eager to offer a means of remembrance to His followers that would last until He returns for the final judgment (1 Cor. 11:26).

WORDS FROM WESLEY

1 Corinthians 11:24

This is my body which is broken for you—That is, this broken bread is the sign of my body, which is even now to be pierced and wounded for your iniquities. Take then and eat of this bread, in a humble, thankful, obediential remembrance of my dying love; of the extremity of my sufferings on your behalf, of the blessings I have thereby procured for you, and of the obligations to love and duty. (ENNT)

Unworthy Behavior (1 Cor. 11:27–32)

Whoever eats the bread or drinks the cup of the Lord in an unworthy manner (v. 27) was a rebuke from Paul, addressing the Corinthian church's sin against the body of Christ, through irreverence. One of the key components is attitude. The church was being reminded that they were not participating in a mindless ritual. When they behaved in this manner, they were sinning against the work of Jesus on the cross, belittling what Jesus had done for them, and mocking Jesus and making light of His sacrifice.

Paul also gave a spiritual directive for self-examination, prior to receiving the elements. Each person should look within his or her own heart and test his or her actions and attitude. In doing so, there is opportunity for repentance through a spiritual means of grace (v. 28). When Paul spoke of **judgment** in verse 29, he was not referring to God's eternal judgment, but to the fact that God sometimes uses physical sickness and even death as a means of discipline. **Have fallen asleep** (v. 30) is a figure of speech commonly used in the first century for death.

Paul reminded the Corinthians that God uses discipline to help us repent of our sins (v. 32). "Godly sorrow brings repentance that leads to salvation and leaves no regret, but worldly sorrow brings death" (2 Cor. 7:10). As God's children, we have to be spiritually disciplined, just as human parents have to discipline their children. Only those who are willing to confess sin in their lives should partake in this sacrament.

WORDS FROM WESLEY

1 Corinthians 11:26

In this world we are never free from temptations. Whatever way of life we are in, whatever our condition be, whether we are sick or well, in trouble or at ease, the enemies of our souls are watching to lead us into sin. And too often they prevail over us. Now, when we are convinced of having sinned against God, what surer way have we of procuring pardon from Him, than the "showing forth the Lord's death"; and beseeching Him, for the sake of His Son's sufferings, to blot out all our sins?

The grace of God given herein confirms to us the pardon of our sins, and enables us to leave them. As our bodies are strengthened by bread and wine, so are our souls by these tokens of the body and the blood of Christ. This is the food of our souls: This gives strength to perform our duty, and leads us on to perfection. If, therefore, we have any regard for the plain command of Christ, if we desire the pardon of our sins, if we wish for strength to believe, to love and obey God, then we should neglect no opportunity of receiving the Lord's Supper; then we must never turn our backs on the feast which our Lord has prepared for us. We must neglect no occasion, which the good providence of God affords us, for this purpose. (WJW, vol. 7, 148)

John Wesley fought hard to retain "open Communion" so anyone could come to the table. He believed part of the purpose of the Supper was conversion. He did not restrict Communion to those who had no sin, but felt it was precisely for those sinners who did not understand. Paul's point here was that the church should understand their sin.

WORDS FROM WESLEY

1 Corinthians 11:28

Only "let a man" first "examine himself," whether he understands the nature and design of this holy institution, and whether he really desires to be himself made conformable to the death of Christ; and so, nothing doubting, "let him eat of that bread, and drink of that cup" (v. 28). (WJW, vol. 5, 194)

Benefit of Waiting (1 Cor. 11:33–34)

In encouraging the Corinthian church to exercise self-restraint, Paul was teaching them a spiritual discipline. **When you come together** (v. 33) means *each* time you gather. He gave a simple directive in one word — **wait**. **Wait for each other**, for order, for the sake of appropriate communion within the body of Christ. **And when I come I will give further directions** (v. 34) indicates that he had more to say on the subject of the Lord's Supper.

Paul offered a refreshing reminder that when we hurry through the ordinance of Communion or take it lightly, without the benefit of self-examination, we risk bringing unholy behavior and sin into the church, and bring God's judgment on ourselves. As Paul reminded the church at Corinth, let us remind ourselves that when we enter Communion, it is a reflection of our relationship with Christ and a reminder of His sacrifice for us.

DISCUSSION

The Lord's Supper is a beautiful sacrament, but what purpose does it serve? Discuss who should partake of the Lord's Supper and what attitude each participant should have.

1. How do you think individual believers should prepare to celebrate the Lord's Supper?

2. Which is your preferred designation: the Lord's Supper, Communion, the Eucharist, the Lord's Table? Explain.

3. Why do divisions at the Lord's Supper make a mockery of the sacrament?

4. How does the Lord's Supper help you remember that all believers share common ground?

5. How would you answer someone who claimed the elements used in Communion were the actual body and blood of the Lord?

6. Must a believer be perfect before he or she partakes of the Lord's Supper? Why or why not?

7. How might someone partake of the Lord's Supper unworthily?

8. How has the Lord's Supper specifically blessed you?

PRAYER

Father God, please help us bring greater unity to the body this week. Let us help each member overcome the externals of their circumstances to find common life in You.

7

UNWRAP YOUR GIFT

1 Corinthians 12:1–11; 12:27—13:1

Seek the Spirit, who gives gifts to His bride, the church.

Have you ever received a wrapped box or package that contained a useless gift? Your wonder and excitement probably fell lower than your jaw when you saw what was inside. Some useless gifts, called white elephant gifts, are often exchanged at parties. They may be nicely gift-wrapped but designed to cause the party guests to laugh. Plastic flowers, an ugly sweater, one chopstick, or a dented hubcap, or unmatched socks qualify as white elephant gifts.

However, as this study points out, spiritual gifts are a far cry from being useless. God gives them to us to use for His glory and the edification of our fellow believers.

COMMENTARY

The Corinthian church was established by Paul in what is now Greece on his second missionary journey. By the time he was nearing the end of his long ministry at Ephesus in Asia Minor during his third missionary journey, the congregation at Corinth was becoming his "problem" church. He dealt with some of the problems in 1 Corinthians, written about A.D. 55. One matter that led to difficulty was spiritual gifts—the various ways in which the Holy Spirit manifests himself in believers for the building up of the church.

Paul dedicated the section beginning in 1 Corinthians 7 to answering questions that had been addressed to him by the

Corinthians (7:1). The answer to one question is given in 1 Corinthians 12–14. Chapter 12 deals with the variety of spiritual gifts. Chapter 13 declares that agape love is greater than spiritual gifts. Chapter 14 shows the superiority of prophecy to language-speaking and talks about proper decorum in worship.

The Inspiration of the Holy Spirit (1 Cor. 12:1–3)

Paul did not want the Corinthians **to be ignorant** (v. 1) about *spirituals* (word in the original). From all he had to say about spiritual gifts in these three chapters, it is obvious that this matter had become a problem. He pointed out that their former pagan life had given evidence of ignorance since **somehow or other you were . . . led astray to mute idols** (v. 2). He did not want ignorance to lead them astray again. He proceeded to enlighten them about the source of two messages. One was **"Jesus be cursed"** (v. 3). It is possible that some demonic activity had made use of such a statement. Paul made it clear that it could not be **by the Spirit of God** (v. 3).

The other message was **"Jesus is Lord"** (v. 3). This was the statement by which converts confessed Christ publicly in those early days. It became a direct challenge to the Romans, because their cry was, "Caesar is lord," and they insisted Christians say that. Christians steadfastly refused and many went to their death as a result. Paul told the Corinthians **no one can say, "Jesus is Lord," except by the Holy Spirit** (v. 3).

The Manifestations of the Holy Spirit (1 Cor. 12:4–7)

Paul began to write about the rich diversity of the Spirit's manifestations. **There are different kinds of gifts, but** it is **the same Spirit** (v. 4) who distributes them to the believers. The power behind the gifts is the Holy Spirit. **There are different kinds of service** (v. 5), but it is **the same Lord** (Jesus) who inspires and blesses believers as they serve one another. **There**

are different kinds of working (v. 6). The word translated
working refers to results. But behind the differences, the same
God works all of them in all men (v. 6). There is an implied
reference to the Trinity here in verses 4–6, only in the reverse of
our normal order—Spirit, Lord, God.

●

WORDS FROM WESLEY

1 Corinthians 12:4

Hence we may observe, that the chief . . . *spiritual gifts*, con-
ferred on the apostolical church, were: (1) casting out devils; (2)
speaking with new tongues; (3) escaping dangers, in which otherwise they must have perished; (4) healing the sick; (5) prophecy,
foretelling things to come; (6) visions; (7) divine dreams; and (8)
discerning of spirits.

Some of these appear to have been chiefly designed for the
conviction of Jews and Heathens—as the casting out devils and
speaking with new tongues; some, chiefly for the benefit of their
fellow-Christians—as healing the sick, foretelling things to come,
and the discernment of spirits; and all, in order to enable those
who either wrought or saw them, to "run with patience the race
set before them," through all the storms of persecution which the
most inveterate prejudice, rage, and malice could raise against
them. (WJW, vol. 10, 16)

Then Paul made a strong statement: to each one the manifestation of the Spirit is given for the common good (v. 7). He was
plainly saying every Christian has some manifestation of the Holy
Spirit by which he or she serves the Christian fellowship. Every
Christian has at least one gift (Rom. 12:3–6; 1 Cor. 12:11, 27; Eph.
4:7; 1 Pet. 4:10). They are given for the purpose of blessing fellow
believers (Rom. 12:5–10, 13, 16; 1 Cor. 12:12, 25–26, 31; 13:1–13;
14:1, 3–5, 12; Eph. 4:2–3, 11–16; 1 Pet. 4:8, 10). According to
1 Corinthians 12:4–6, the Spirit, the Lord, and God are behind our
ministries, making it clear that spiritual gifts are to be used in divine
power (Rom. 12:11; 1 Cor. 12:8–11; Eph. 4:3–6; 1 Pet. 4:11).

The Various Workings of the Holy Spirit (1 Cor. 12:8–11)

Then Paul began to discuss specific gifts. Some he mentioned here are not mentioned in other New Testament passages. Even when we put all biblical references to gifts together, we have no indication that this is an exhaustive list. The first Paul mentioned is **the message of wisdom** (v. 8). **Wisdom** is not the same as knowledge, but is the practical application of knowledge. A wise word spoken when a religious body is deliberating can relieve differences of opinion and speed a decision leading to action.

He followed this with **the message of knowledge** (v. 8). This implies study and learning, although Paul also used **knowledge** with reference to divine revelation and special insights granted by the Spirit (1 Cor. 13:2, 8–9, 12; 14:6, 26). It is closely related to "teaching" (Rom. 12:7; 1 Cor. 12:28–29; Eph. 4:11).

Then Paul mentioned **faith** (1 Cor. 12:9) as a gift. Jesus had assured His disciples that faith the size of a mustard seed would be adequate to move mountains (Matt. 17:20–21). But Paul seemed to have said some Christians are given a special gift of faith beyond that of other believers. (Faith is also referred to in 1 Cor. 13:2, 13).

Paul moved on to **gifts of healing** (12:9). Jesus healed many in His ministry, but He had to help His followers concentrate on His teaching rather than being completely taken up with healing. Peter, John, and Paul were used in healing ministries. While divine healing is not limited to those with the gifts of healing, there have been and are those especially gifted for such a ministry. He also mentioned **miraculous powers** (v. 10). These seem to refer to miracles other than healings.

Then came **prophecy** (v. 10; also in Rom. 12:6 and Eph. 4:11). This was a gift Paul valued highly as he referred to it in 13:2, 8–9, and throughout chapter 14. This would involve foretelling future events (Acts 11:27–28; 21:10–11), but it was not limited to this. The Old Testament prophets had foretold the future, but their main ministry was *forth-telling*, preaching God's will for His people. So prophecy in the New Testament and today involves repeating God's message to His people.

Paul spoke of **distinguishing between spirits** (1 Cor. 12:10) as a spiritual gift. John later exhorted people to "test the spirits" in a time when many false teachers were attempting to pervert the gospel (1 John 4:1–6). This is something every Christian must do to a certain extent. But provision has been made by the Holy Spirit for gifted specialists to aid the church in this matter.

Next Paul mentioned two related gifts: **speaking in different kinds of tongues** (languages) and **the interpretation of tongues** (1 Cor. 12:10). First Corinthians 12–14 is the only place in the New Testament where these are discussed as gifts. In Acts, there are three instances in which groups of believers spoke in languages they had not known: at Pentecost (Acts 2:4–15), at Cornelius's house (Acts 10:44–48), and at Ephesus by twelve whom Paul met (Acts 19:1–7).

The passage on the Pentecost occasion makes it clear that what were spoken were actual languages not previously known by the speakers but understood by the hearers (Acts 2:5–12). Peter was explicit in saying what happened at Cornelius's house was the same thing that happened at Pentecost (Acts 10:47; 11:15–17). There is nothing at Ephesus to suggest anything different. There is nothing in 1 Corinthians 12–14 that necessitates the interpretation that what happened at Corinth in language-speaking was any different from the accounts in Acts.

The Roman Empire was a multi-language conglomerate. Latin was the language of law and government, and Greek the language of commerce. But people needed to hear the gospel in their native languages, and God provided supernatural means to make that possible. The one gift provided for persons to be empowered by the Holy Spirit to *preach* in languages they had not previously learned. The other provided for persons to be empowered by the Holy Spirit to *translate* languages they had not previously learned. Examples of these gifts for the purpose of sharing the gospel can be found among missionaries, even in modern times. It is interesting to note that there is nothing in the writings of the early church fathers to connect the language-speaking of 1 Corinthians 12–14 with ecstatic speech, non-speech, or a special prayer language.

WORDS FROM WESLEY
1 Corinthians 12:11

As he willeth—The Greek word does not so much imply arbitrary pleasure, as a determination founded on wise counsel. (ENNT)

The Distribution of the Spirit's Gifts (1 Cor. 12:27–30)

In 12:27, Paul summarized what he had said in 12:12–26: **Now you are the body of Christ, and each one of you is a part of it.** And then he talked about the variety of Holy Spirit manifestations in powerful ministry through the members. He spoke of God having **appointed** (v. 28) each one. This time he began with three office gifts also mentioned in Ephesians 4:11. The **apostles** (1 Cor. 12:28) were the "sent ones," messengers who opened the world to the gospel, somewhat as missionaries today, only on a broader scale. The **prophets** (v. 10) were those messengers of God who had the gift of prophecy. The **teachers** (v. 28) are mentioned in Ephesians 4:11 in conjunction with pastors; there the best translation would be hyphenated as pastor-teachers. **Workers of miracles** and **those** with **gifts of healing** (1 Cor. 12:28) were covered in the earlier list. He mentioned two not given before: **those able to help others** (v. 28) with the special gift of being able to assist fellow believers in countless ways (called "serving" in Rom. 12:7) and **those with gifts of administration** (1 Cor. 12:28)—those who have the abilities of leadership (called "leadership" in Rom. 12:8). And again Paul mentioned **those speaking in different kinds of tongues** (1 Cor. 12:28).

WORDS FROM WESLEY

1 Corinthians 12:28

First apostles—Who plant the gospel in the heathen nations: *Secondly, prophets*—Who either foretell things to come, or speak by extraordinary inspiration, for the edification of the church: *Thirdly, teachers*, who precede even those that work miracles. Under prophets and teachers, are comprised evangelists and pastors (Eph. 4:11), *helps, governments*—It does not appear that these mean distinct offices. Rather, any persons might be called helps, from a peculiar dexterity in helping the distressed; and governments, from a peculiar talent for governing or presiding in assemblies. (ENNT)

Finally, Paul made it clear with a series of questions that there is no spiritual gift that all believers have. Each of the questions in 12:29–30 begins with a Greek word for *no* or *not*, which is used at the beginning of a question to which a negative answer is expected: **Are all apostles? Are all prophets? Are all teachers? Do all work miracles? Do all have gifts of healing? Do all speak in tongues? Do all interpret?** The expected answer in each case is no. Just as the physical body is made up of not one but many parts, so the spiritual body is made up of not one but many spiritual gifts.

The True Evidence of the Spirit (1 Cor. 12:31—13:1)

Paul then exhorted them to desire **the greater gifts** (12:31). Apparently, the Corinthians had been impressed with the spectacular gifts, particularly the language-speaking and interpreting. Paul had called them "worldly" in 1 Corinthians 3:1–3 ("carnal" in the KJV). They were desiring gifts that would give them prominence, that seemed to them to represent the most remarkable power. Paul used much of 1 Corinthians 14 to point out the superiority of prophecy to language-speaking. It is possible some of the people were producing their own version of language-speaking, not that provided by the Holy Spirit. Paul was calling them in 1 Corinthians 14 to communicate intelligibly so the hearers could be edified.

Then he said, **I will show you the most excellent way** (12:31), so beginning one of his greatest chapters—the love chapter. He began by saying, **If I speak in the tongues of men and of angels**—exaggerating for the sake of emphasis—**but have not love, I am only a resounding gong or a clanging cymbal** (13:1). Rather than the bickering and quarreling, jostling for position and recognition that had been going on, the great need of the Corinthian church was agape love. Love was the true evidence of the Holy Spirit's presence and power. It took precedence over all the gifts and was essential to their proper implementation.

WORDS FROM WESLEY
1 Corinthians 12:31

In the preceding verses, St. Paul has been speaking of the extraordinary gifts of the Holy Ghost; such as healing the sick; prophesying, in the proper sense of the word, that is, foretelling things to come; speaking with strange tongues, such as the speaker had never learned; and the miraculous interpretation of tongues. And these gifts the apostle allows to be desirable; yea, he exhorts the Corinthians, at least the teachers among them (to whom chiefly, if not solely, they were wont to be given in the first ages of the church), to *covet* them *earnestly*, that thereby they might be qualified to be more useful either to Christians or Heathens. "And yet," says he, "I show unto you a more excellent way"; far more desirable than all these put together: Inasmuch as it will infallibly lead you to happiness, both in this world and in the world to come; whereas you might have all those gifts, yea, in the highest degree, and yet be miserable both in time and eternity. (WJW, vol. 7, 26)

DISCUSSION

Presents can make a birthday or Christmas exciting. However, unwrapping a birthday or Christmas gift is not as exciting as discovering the spiritual gift or gifts God has given you.

1. Read 1 Corinthians 12:1–2. In what way(s) did ignorance of spiritual matters lead you astray before you became a believer?

2. Why do you agree or disagree that spiritual gifts are different from talents?

3. Is it possible for a congregation of believers to have no spiritual gifts? Why or why not?

4. How have you seen spiritual gifts manifested in your life? In your church?

5. Do you think speaking in tongues (languages) was something the Corinthians needed to obtain by some effort? Why or why not?

6. According to 1 Corinthians 13:1, what should the attitude of believers be toward the application of spiritual gifts without love?

PRAYER

God, we pray for Your help to better use the spiritual gifts You have given us to build up others and to glorify You.

8

WORSHIP THAT HONORS GOD

1 Corinthians 14:24–40

Worship should reflect God's presence.

Something beautiful and pleasing seems to be associated with order. God created an orderly world and saw that it was good. An orderly classroom delights a teacher. When our cars run in good order, we are happy. But disorder causes frustration and disappointment.

How do we worship? If our worship is orderly, it is beautiful and pleasing not only to us, but also to God.

COMMENTARY

The concerns Paul addressed in the letter we call 1 Corinthians may have been issues that had been put in writing and sent to Paul, or the questions may have been delivered orally. Divisions in the church were a concern in 1:10–17. In chapter 12, Paul again addressed the issue of divisions, acknowledging diversity among the members. He described the church as a unified body of members who had different gifts. The members performed different functions in the church, but all were designed by the Spirit to edify the whole body and thereby bring glory to God. Paul gave more perspective in chapter 13 when he discussed the Christian virtues of faith, hope, and love. He declared that love is "the most excellent" of all the gifts of the Spirit. Love will both outlast the gifts and any benefits to be gained from the gifts.

In chapter 14, Paul moved on to the issue of worship. If only Paul would tell us what type of worship is God-ordained: whether traditional, contemporary, blended, liturgical, or formless worship is most pleasing to God. Though he is not here, Paul did lay down guidelines that may be helpful.

Included among Paul's guidelines are the following: (1) Worship should be orderly; (2) it should be understandable to the initiated (the believer) and the uninitiated (the nonbeliever); (3) in worship one person should speak at a time; (4) the role of women in worship should not be disruptive (neither should men); (5) we should desire the ability to prophesy in worship. Perhaps we can apply Paul's guidelines to our present-day dilemmas about worship.

In the first half of chapter 14, Paul dealt primarily with the issue of speaking in tongues as a part of worship. Whether the tongues Paul referred to are unknown or actually foreign languages is less important than the guidelines Paul gave for dealing with the issue:

- Unless there is an interpreter, tongues only edify the person speaking and not the hearers (14:1–5).
- We should seek gifts that build up the church (14:6–13).
- We should always pray that God will enable us to understand the words we speak or pray. Otherwise it does not edify ourselves nor anyone else (14:13–17).
- Paul spoke in many tongues, but his stated purpose was to speak "intelligible words to instruct others" (14:19).
- If the whole church speaks in tongues and unbelievers come in, "will they not say that you are out of your mind?" (14:23).

There is plenty of evidence that Paul did not believe tongues are "the sign" of the baptism of the Spirit and that he did not believe tongues should be an important aspect of ordinary worship. We will return to this issue briefly when we look at verses 39–40.

The Value of Prophecy in Worship (1 Cor. 14:24–25)

After addressing the issue of the use of tongues in worship, Paul turned to broader aspects of worship. **But if an unbeliever or someone who does not understand comes in while everybody is prophesying, he will be convinced by all that he is a sinner and will be judged by all, and the secrets of his heart will be laid bare. So he will fall down and worship God, exclaiming, "God is really among you!"** (vv. 24–25).

In contrast to the use of tongues in worship, Paul discussed the effect of prophesying on a person who is an unbeliever or an inquirer. What is prophecy? Though prophecy in the New Testament sometimes means prediction, it usually refers to insightful preaching that reveals the truth. Thus, if a believer is truly prophesying, the unbeliever will be convicted of secret sins and will acknowledge God's presence. Prophesying brings conviction that will lead to repentance if the sinner does not harden his or her heart. This contrasts with the pronouncement of madness for worshipers involved in unrestrained use of tongues.

Paul seemed to consider prophecy one of the more important gifts of the Spirit (1 Cor. 12:28–31; 14:39). Through prophecy, God is revealed to the hearts of sinful men and women. Martin Luther believed the church should be a *mund* (or mouth) house—a place for preaching God's Word (prophesying). Protestants have a strong scriptural mandate for making the preaching of the Word central in worship settings. Church architecture that makes the pulpit central is one way to symbolize that emphasis physically.

The Purpose of Other Elements of Worship (1 Cor. 14:26–28)

What then shall we say, brothers? When you come together, everyone has a hymn, or a word of instruction, a revelation, a tongue or an interpretation. All of these must be done for the strengthening of the church. If anyone speaks in a tongue,

two—or at the most three—should speak, one at a time, and someone must interpret (vv. 26–27).

Though prophecy may be central in worship, its position does not detract from the importance of other aspects of worship. Music, teaching, and sometimes a fresh revelation from God all have a legitimate place. A hymn can be interpreted to mean Old Testament Psalms or other kinds of music. To interpret hymns narrowly in either direction would be a mistake.

WORDS FROM WESLEY

1 Corinthians 14:26

What a thing is it, brethren—This was another disorder among them. *Every one hath a psalm*—That is, at the same time one begins to sing a psalm: another to deliver a doctrine; another to speak in an unknown tongue; another to declare what has been revealed in him, another to interpret what the former is speaking: every one probably gathering a little company about him, just as they did in the schools of the philosophers. *Let all be done to edification*—So as to profit [all] the hearers. (ENNT)

Further insight may be gained from Paul's words in Ephesians 5:19–20: "Speak to one another with psalms, hymns and spiritual songs. Sing and make music in your heart to the Lord, always giving thanks to God the Father for everything, in the name of our Lord Jesus Christ." The attitude of the heart is a central aspect in worship and probably is more important than the particular type of music we sing.

Teaching is another important element. One of the most important tasks of the church is instruction, and that includes instruction within worship. Perhaps the most important task of the pastor is instruction, but others may be involved, as well. Testimonies of believers, dramas, sermons, and other methods can be vehicles for instruction. Paul referred to spontaneous exhortation as **a word of instruction** (1 Cor. 14:26), which may certainly have its place in modern worship settings.

Some of us may feel less certain about **a revelation** (v. 26). However, it is clear that, in the New Testament church, the Spirit sometimes revealed new insights to the believers. We still pray that God will reveal His will and will call believers into His work, both of which are types of revelation. Certainly we believe any new revelation from God will not contradict the Bible. Nevertheless, we need God's direction related to decisions that must continually be made within the church. Today we have generally accepted the consensus of the group or the majority vote to represent that revelation. Perhaps words of revelation from God's saints would also be **for the strengthening of the church** (1 Cor. 14:26).

Paul returned to tongues in worship. If someone speaks in a tongue, there must be an interpreter. Furthermore, no more than two or at most three should speak in tongues. Apparently this means in any one worship setting. If no interpreter comes forward, then no tongues should be used. **The speaker should keep quiet in the church and speak to himself and God** (v. 28).

WORDS FROM WESLEY

1 Corinthians 14:27

By two or three at most—Let not above two or three speak at one meeting; *and that by course*—That is, one after another; *and let one interpret*—Either himself (v. 13) or (if he have not the gift) some other, into the vulgar [common] tongue. It seems the gift or tongues was an instantaneous knowledge of a tongue till then unknown, which he that received it, could afterward speak when he thought fit, without any new miracle. (ENNT)

The Orderly Use of Gifts in Worship (1 Cor. 14:29–35)

Two or three prophets should speak, and the others should weigh carefully what is said. And if a revelation comes to someone who is sitting down, the first speaker should stop (vv. 29–30).

Though Paul favored the gift of prophecy, he wanted prophets to be orderly. In one gathering, no more than two or three prophets should speak, and that should be done one at a time. If one prophet is speaking when another feels inspired, the first one should stop and give the next prophet the floor. **You can all prophesy in turn so that everyone may be instructed and encouraged** (v. 31). True prophets are **subject to the control of prophets** (v. 32). If someone is not willing to be submissive to the prophets, there is something questionable about his or her revelation. Discernment and consensus are important for the church and for worship.

WORDS FROM WESLEY
1 Corinthians 14:32

The Spirit of God left His prophets the clear use of their judgment, when and how long it was fit for them to speak, and never hurried them into any improprieties, either as to the matter, manner, or time of their speaking. (ENNT)

Paul then gave a major principle for worship: **For God is not a God of disorder but of peace** (v. 33). This principle applies to everyone and every part of worship. Order and peace should always be present. There have been times when this principle seems to have been overlooked. Some of the services of John Wesley manifested disorder, but Wesley always spoke calmly and discouraged such "enthusiasm." Likewise, country frontier revivals and camp meetings often were not orderly. Wesley followed Paul's advice as did most leaders in American revivals. Thus, order was restored before long.

We should question leaders or movements that do not take Paul's words to heart and encourage order in worship. This is not to say emotionalism is never appropriate when some persons are convicted or when other persons are blessed. However, uncontrolled emotionalism contradicts Paul's guideline. Like Wesley and others, we may be puzzled by extreme emotionalism, but we should never retreat from our insistence on order in worship. If we do, we dishonor our God, for he is the **God . . . of peace** (v. 33).

As in all the congregations of the saints, women should remain silent in the churches. They are not allowed to speak, but must be in submission, as the Law says. If they want to inquire about something, they should ask their own husbands at home; for it is disgraceful for a woman to speak in the church (vv. 33–35).

Here we have a statement from Paul that has divided Bible interpreters. It is clear from 1 Corinthians 11:5 that women did pray and prophesy, presumably in worship gatherings. So what did Paul mean? Some believe this passage, along with 1 Timothy 2:11–14, forbids women to ever teach or lead in worship. Other traditions do not agree with that restriction, because of several other passages that present a different message. Some interpreters have guessed that women would occasionally speak out in worship in a disruptive way, asking questions. We should keep in mind that the New Testament gatherings for worship were usually in a house rather than in a formal sanctuary. In spite of the informality of the setting, Paul said they should ask their questions later. It seems Paul was still calling for orderliness in worship.

Concluding Remarks (1 Cor. 14:36–40)

Did the word of God originate with you? Or are you the only people it has reached? If anybody thinks he is a prophet

or spiritually gifted, let him acknowledge that what I am writing to you is the Lord's command. If he ignores this, he himself will be ignored (vv. 36–38).

Some of the congregation at Corinth apparently resisted Paul's authority, and this passage seems to focus on them. Paul believed he had given the Lord's command, and they should acknowledge his authority. Christianity is not an individualistic religion. Believers are members of a body, and even prophets should be subject to the authority of the church and its leaders. If anyone disagreed with Paul's instruction, he or she should be ignored.

Therefore, my brothers, be eager to prophesy, and do not forbid speaking in tongues. But everything should be done in a fitting and orderly way (vv. 39–40).

Paul concluded this section on the conduct of worship by encouraging prophecy by believers. Still he did not forbid other gifts, including speaking in tongues. The gifts the Spirit gives are to build up the church (1 Cor. 12:7). Paul reminded them that order should prevail in worship no matter what gifts may be manifested.

WORDS FROM WESLEY

1 Corinthians 14:40

Decently—By every individual: *in order*—By the whole church. (ENNT)

DISCUSSION

Worship has become one of the most controversial subjects in the modern church. But what does the Bible have to say about worship? Let us always be sure that our worship is God-honoring and pleasing to Him.

1. How do you define genuine worship?

2. Why do you agree or disagree that worship is solely the responsibility of the church's paid staff?

3. What comments from visitors has your church's worship received?

4. How can you personally contribute to worship that glorifies God and edifies fellow believers?

5. What kind of music heightens your worship experience? Why?

6. Why do you agree or disagree that an orderly worship service benefits those who attend?

7. Why do you agree or disagree that worship services should be planned instead of spontaneous?

PRAYER

Almighty God, You are indeed worthy of our praise, thoughts, obedience, and worship. Train our hearts to bless You each moment.

9

BECAUSE HE LIVES

1 Corinthians 15:1–20

Sin and death are defeated enemies because of
the resurrection of Christ.

A tombstone inscription in a cemetery in Ruidoso, New Mexico, reads: "Here lies Johnny Yeast. Pardon me for not rising." If Mr. Yeast requested this inscription while he was alive, he certainly had a sense of humor. However, he and all the dead will rise. Jesus promised: "A time is coming when all who are in their graves will hear his voice and come out" (John 5:28–29).

This study assures us that Jesus died and rose from the dead. Because He lives, we too will live. Death cannot hold us. As our study emphasizes, this is good news to be cherished and shared.

COMMENTARY

First Corinthians 15 is one of the longest chapters in all of Paul's letters, and it is devoted to a discussion of the resurrection of the body from the dead. This study focuses on just a portion of this chapter.

It appears some Corinthian believers were denying the doctrine, asserting that there is "no resurrection from the dead" (15:12). Greek thought commonly denied the resurrection of the body. In Athens a few years before writing this letter, Paul had proclaimed the resurrection of Jesus from the dead, and Luke said "some sneered" at him (Acts 17:32). Generally, Greeks believed the soul or spirit is good and immortal. Plato and many Greeks believed the soul would be reincarnated in different bodies over an extended period of time. On the other hand, the Greeks did not consider the body as good. Rather the body was the prison dragging the soul down from its highest purpose. Thus, the idea of the resurrection of the body went against the worldview of the Greeks. It is no wonder that denial of the resurrection arose in a Greek city like Corinth.

However, Paul and other early apostles were clear that the resurrection of Jesus was fundamental to the Christian faith. It is central in the sermons in Acts, providing proof that Jesus was the Messiah or Christ as promised in the Old Testament. Furthermore, the resurrection of Jesus was positive proof that Christian believers would be resurrected from the dead. Hebrew and Christian thought always affirm the goodness of the body, and both religious groups believe the complete human person requires body and spirit united. A disembodied soul was not a complete human person. Furthermore, for Christians the resurrection of Jesus and His ascension into heaven demonstrated the value of both body and spirit.

Thus, Paul addressed the resurrection of the body as the final issue in this letter to the Corinthian believers. They had many questions and mistaken ideas, including questions about the resurrection of the dead. However, this doctrine was vital to their faith in Christ, and Paul left no doubt that the resurrection of the dead was a certainty for Christian believers.

The Centrality of the Resurrection (1 Cor. 15:1–8)

Now, brothers, I want to remind you of the gospel I preached to you, which you received and on which you have taken your stand. By this gospel you are saved, if you hold firmly to the word I preached to you. Otherwise, you have believed in vain (vv. 1–2).

Some people believe that doctrine is not important, but Paul disagreed. Paul declared the resurrection of the body cannot be separated from the gospel message without destroying that message.

He declared that we must accept certain teachings to be saved. If we try to shape the gospel message to suit ourselves or to match popular ideas, we are in danger of perverting the message. Paul's exhortation was to **hold firmly to the word I preached to you. Otherwise, you have believed in vain** (v. 2).

For what I received I passed on to you as of first importance: that Christ died for our sins according to the Scriptures, that he was buried, that he was raised on the third day according to the Scriptures and that he appeared to Peter, and then to the Twelve (vv. 3–5).

Paul received the gospel message from others, and he passed it on to the Corinthians. Of first importance in the gospel message were three facts: (1) **Christ died for our sins**; (2) **he was buried**, as proof of His death; and (3) **he** rose again **on the third day**. But these were not fact-claims no one could corroborate. There were witnesses who saw all three facts. Peter and the twelve apostles (including Matthias) had been witnesses. Others also witnessed the resurrection. Paul said the resurrected Lord **appeared to more than five hundred of the brothers at the same time, most of whom are still living. Then he appeared to James, then to all the apostles, and last of all he appeared to me also, as to one abnormally born** (vv. 6–8). Paul was not simply passing on tales, for there were numerous living witnesses who could attest to the resurrection of Jesus.

WORDS FROM WESLEY

1 Corinthians 15:4

According to the Scriptures—He proves it first from Scripture, then from the testimony of a cloud of witnesses. (ENNT)

Paul's Personal Reflection on His Rebirth (1 Cor. 15:9–10)

For I am the least of the apostles and do not even deserve to be called an apostle, because I persecuted the church of God (v. 9).

Perhaps Paul called himself "abnormally born" (v. 8) because he was not one of the apostles who were with Jesus during His earthly ministry. His apostleship was abnormal in that sense. Also, as a witness of the resurrection, he had seen the risen Lord at a later time, traveling on the road to Damascus. Paul also stated that he had no right to be an apostle, having **persecuted the church of God. But by the grace of God I am what I am, and his grace to me was not without effect. No, I worked harder than all of them—yet not I, but the grace of God that was with me** (vv. 9–10). Despite Paul's sinful past, God had done a work of grace in him that enabled him as he worked harder. Yet it was not Paul who was working through his own strength; rather it was the grace of God working in and through Paul. Paul was careful to make sure all praise went to God.

WORDS FROM WESLEY
1 Corinthians 15:9

I persecuted the church—True believers are humbled all their lives, even for the sins they committed before they believed. (ENNT)

Proclaiming the Resurrection (1 Cor. 15:11–20)

Paul returned to the main subject of the chapter in verse 11: **Whether, then, it was I or they, this is what we preach, and this is what you believed.** Paul and other apostles preached the resurrection, then the Corinthians believed the message. Now they should not be tempted to listen to people who doubted whether the resurrection of the body was possible. Popular ideas in culture are often attractive and persuasive. As believers, we must be grounded on the teachings of Scripture, not tuned to the latest popular ideas.

But if it is preached that Christ has been raised from the dead, how can some of you say that there is no resurrection of the dead? (v. 12).

Paul had cited numerous personal witnesses as evidence for the resurrection of Jesus. This is evidence that resurrection of the body does occur. If the testimony was considered credible, it was strong evidence. In this section, Paul turned to a powerful argument from logic. Through his argument, he demonstrated that Christians must not agree with those who deny the resurrection of the body. He gave seven points in his argument beginning with verse 12.

First, **if it is preached that Christ has been raised from the dead** (v. 12), then resurrection of the dead must be possible. To deny the possibility of resurrection is to deny the preaching of the gospel.

Second, **if there is no resurrection of the dead, then not even Christ has been raised** (v. 13). The heart of the gospel message was that Christ has risen. Witnessing to the resurrection was the assignment Jesus gave the eleven apostles before He ascended to the Father (Acts 1:7–9). Christ's resurrection was the main point of sermons preached by Peter on the day of Pentecost (Acts 2), by Paul at Pisidian Antioch (Acts 13:14), and by Paul at Athens (Acts 17:16–31). A denial of the resurrection cut the heart out of the Christian proclamation.

Third, **if Christ has not been raised, our preaching is useless and so is your faith** (1 Cor. 15:14). Not only would the gospel message be destroyed, but Christian faith would also be destroyed because it is based on the gospel. There is nothing on which to base our faith without the resurrection of Christ. Paul did not agree with the position of modern theologians who would make faith all that matters for the Christian. For Christian faith to be adequate, there must be a historical basis.

Fourth, **we are then found to be false witnesses about God, for we have testified about God that he raised Christ from the dead. But he did not raise him if in fact the dead are not raised** (v. 15). The apostles would be spreading false teachings, and all their preaching would be in error, misleading believers. If this were true, the most respected leaders of the church were deliberately teaching falsehoods, or else they were mistaken in their beliefs.

WORDS FROM WESLEY

1 Corinthians 15:17

Ye are still in your sins—That is, under the guilt of them. So that there needed something more than reformation (which was plainly wrought), in order to their being delivered from the guilt of sin: even that atonement, the sufficiency of which God attested, by raising our great Surety from the grave. (ENNT)

Fifth, **if the dead are not raised, then Christ has not been raised either. And if Christ has not been raised, your faith is futile; you are still in your sins** (vv. 16–17). Most devastating of all, without the resurrection, believers have not been delivered from their sins. They stand guilty and lost.

Sixth, **those also who have fallen asleep in Christ are lost** (v. 18). Furthermore, those believers who have already died are lost. They died in their mistaken belief, and their hope was false and in vain.

Finally, **if only for this life we have hope in Christ, we are to be pitied more than all men** (v. 19). If there is no resurrection, Christianity is a farce. It has nothing to offer, and believers are miserable, misled, hopeless people, lost in their sins. As they face opposition and persecution, Christians are unhappy people living under a delusion. Thus, Paul laid out a detailed argument developed from the original premise that there is no resurrection from the dead. But, praise God, the argument is flawed from the beginning.

WORDS FROM WESLEY

1 Corinthians 15:19

If in this life only we have hope—If we look for nothing beyond the grave. But if we have a divine evidence of things not seen, if we have a hope full of immortality, if we now taste of the powers of the world to come, and see the crown that fadeth not away: then notwithstanding all our present trials, we are more happy than all men. (ENNT)

But Christ has indeed been raised from the dead, the first-fruits of those who have fallen asleep (v. 20).

Thank God the premises of the argument above are wrong. The resurrection of Christ's body has occurred, and His resurrection is proof that resurrection of the dead does occur. The denial of the resurrection is false, and the resurrection of the body has occurred. Furthermore, the resurrection of Christ is the evidence that those who have died in Christ, both past and future, will also rise from the dead. **Christ** is **the firstfruits** of the dead (v. 20).

Thus, Paul affirmed this central doctrine of the Christian faith. People in Corinth questioned the truth of the resurrection. People in the twenty-first century still question it, but the doctrine is the foundation of our hope. We must never waver in our affirmation of this foundational truth. Christ is risen! He is risen, indeed!

DISCUSSION

The resurrection of Jesus Christ was a cardinal truth proclaimed by the apostles. Indeed, Paul's life was transformed when the risen Son of God appeared to him on the road to Damascus.

1. According to 1 Corinthians 15:3–5, what central truths comprise the gospel?

2. How did you first learn that Jesus arose from the dead? How has the fact that He rose changed your life?

3. How would you answer a skeptic who asked how you know Jesus is alive?

4. How are the resurrection and the forgiveness of sins related?

5. Read Romans 3:25. How are the resurrection and justification related?

6. Do you agree or disagree that it is pointless for churches to exist if they do not believe in the resurrection?

7. How does the fact that Christ rose from the dead calm your fear of dying?

8. How does the resurrection help you cope with daily challenges and world tensions?

PRAYER

Lord, the reality of Your resurrection reminds us that we can live each day with confidence. Let us encourage others with that reality and thank You for it.

10

TREASURES IN JARS OF CLAY

2 Corinthians 4:1–18

God shows His glory through frail human beings.

Burglars are thorough in their quest for valuables, but Internet sites suggest unlikely hiding spots. For example, would a burglar look inside a toy in a child's toy box or in a bag of frozen food in which valuables have replaced the frozen contents and the bag has been resealed with glue? The bottom of a can of flour or a hollowed-out furniture leg might be suitable hiding places. Obviously none of these hiding places are foolproof, but one thing is certain: It's what's inside that counts.

This study challenges us to realize that what's inside us is a priceless treasure. It is the gospel, and it is in "jars of clay." However, this treasure is for sharing.

COMMENTARY

The Corinthian church proved to be Paul's most difficult church and led to a series of visits and letters to the congregation. First and 2 Corinthians are the only two letters that have survived, but Paul mentioned others.

The first one is mentioned in 1 Corinthians 5:9–11, written from Ephesus, probably about three years after Paul had left Corinth. It advised the Corinthians not to associate with immoral people.

Afterward some from Chloe's household visited Paul in Ephesus and reported about divisions in the Corinthian church (1 Cor. 1:11–12). About the same time Stephanas, Fortunatus, and Achaicus from Corinth visited Paul (1 Cor. 16:17–18). They may have carried a letter from Corinth that asked Paul several questions (1 Cor. 7:1).

Paul then wrote 1 Corinthians, answering their questions, beginning at 7:1 and running through most of the rest of the letter. First Corinthians was probably delivered to the church by Timothy (1 Cor. 4:17; 16:10).

The report came back that things were getting worse at Corinth. Paul left Ephesus for what he referred to as a "painful visit" to Corinth (2 Cor. 2:1).

Paul returned to Ephesus and wrote a "sorrowful letter" to the Corinthians (2 Cor. 2:3–4). He sent it by Titus.

Paul grew concerned over Titus's slowness to return. He traveled to Troas and then on to Macedonia to try to find Titus (2 Cor. 2:12–13; 7:5–7). Titus met him in Macedonia, and Paul was encouraged by what Titus reported.

Paul then wrote 2 Corinthians from Macedonia (2 Cor. 8:1; 9:2) and indicated he would be coming for a third visit. Titus and others were sent with this letter to prepare for Paul's coming (2 Cor. 8:16–24; 13:1).

Paul's third visit was recorded in Acts 20:1–3.

The problems at Corinth were many. The members were not spiritually mature (1 Cor. 3:1ff.) and became embroiled in all kinds of controversies among themselves. Some were skeptical about Paul's ministry and motives and undermined his influence in the church. Paul dealt with much of this in 2 Corinthians. In chapters 1–7, he wrote about his ministry—its nature, its tribulation, and its great rewards. In chapters 8–9, he promoted the great offering being collected among the Gentile churches to assist the poor Christians in Jerusalem. In chapters 10–13, he gave an impassioned defense of his apostleship. Second Corinthians was Paul's most personal letter. He told us much about himself. The number of uses of first-person pronouns and verbs is astounding.

In the KJV, there are 220 uses of first-person singular words, including his name and *I*, *me*, *myself*, *mine*, and *my*. There are also 231 uses of first-person plural words, including *we*, *us*, *our*, *ours*, and *ourselves*. Second Corinthians 4 was in the center of Paul's writing about his ministry. While he was talking about his service as an apostle, much of what he shared has a legitimate application to every earnest Christian who seeks to glorify the Lord.

The Nature of the Apostles' Ministry (2 Cor. 4:1–6)

Paul began by saying that it is **through God's mercy we have this ministry** (v. 1). With all the difficulties that accompanied his ministry, one might be surprised that Paul said it came through mercy. But he was always intensely aware of God's mercy after his encounter with Jesus on the road to Damascus. He who had persecuted Jesus' followers considered it not only to be mercy that God saved him, but that God chose him to carry the gospel to the Gentiles. And since it was by God's mercy, **we do not lose heart** (v. 1).

Paul had been accused by his adversaries at Corinth of having questionable motives and methods in his ministry. In verses 2–5, Paul answered by listing some things he did not do in his ministry. **We have renounced secret and shameful ways** (v. 2). While answering his adversaries, Paul was probably also referring to their motives and methods.

We do not use deception (v. 2). Paul did not use trickery to win people to the Lord. Jesus' opponents had often tried to lay traps for Jesus with loaded questions and always suffered the consequences due to His amazing answers. Paul did not stoop to such.

Nor do we distort the word of God (v. 2). He neither added to nor subtracted from nor in any way altered God's message. Paul's intention was **setting forth the truth plainly** (v. 2). In so doing, he was commending himself **to every man's conscience in the**

sight of God (v. 2)—appealing to the best in his hearers and trusting God to seal the truth. Apparently his opponents had claimed Paul did not make the gospel clear. But he responded, **if our gospel is veiled, it is veiled to those who are perishing** (v. 3).

WORDS FROM WESLEY

2 Corinthians 4:2

But have renounced—Set at open defiance, *the hidden things of shame*—All things which men need to hide or be ashamed of; *not walking in craftiness*—Using no disguise, subtlety, guile; nor privily corrupting the pure word of God, by any additions or alterations, or by attempting to accommodate it to the taste of the hearers. (ENNT)

Paul had referred in the previous chapter to the veil Moses had put over his face after reflecting the glory of God he had seen on Mount Sinai. Paul said a veil still covered the old covenant for the Jews (2 Cor. 3:12–18). Now he said there is a veil for the Gentiles too, because **the god of this age has blinded the minds of unbelievers** (4:4).

Satan is also called "the prince of this world" (John 12:31; 14:30) and "the ruler of the kingdom of the air" (Eph. 2:2). His power is limited but still enormous. Those who refused to believe the gospel opened the way for Satan to blind them. Those who were blinded **cannot see the light of the gospel of the glory of Christ** (2 Cor. 4:4). This is the first of two eloquent descriptions of the light Paul made (vv. 4, 8). He spoke of Christ as **the image of God** (v. 4). This is a theme Paul expanded on in Colossians 1:15–20. The writer to the Hebrews developed it even more in Hebrews 1:3, where he said, "The Son is the radiance of God's glory and the exact representation of his being" (also John 14:9).

Paul declared, **we do not preach ourselves, but Jesus Christ as Lord** (2 Cor. 4:5). Rather than exalting himself, Paul spoke of himself and others like him as the people's **servants** (literally, "slaves") **for Jesus' sake** (v. 5). In his reference to God letting **light shine out of darkness** (v. 6), he was referring to the creation story (Gen. 1:3). He may also have had in mind the bright light that had arrested him on the road to Damascus and brought him out of personal darkness (Acts 9:3–9). No doubt it applies also to all who have been given **the light of the knowledge of the glory of God in the face of Christ** (2 Cor. 4:6).

WORDS FROM WESLEY

2 Corinthians 4:7

This, invaluable as it is, "we have in earthen vessels." The word is exquisitely proper, denoting both the brittleness of the vessels, and the meanness of the matter they are made of. It directly means, what we term earthenware; china, porcelain, and the like. How weak, how easily broken in pieces! Just such is the case with a holy Christian. We have the heavenly treasure in earthly, mortal, corruptible bodies. "Dust thou art," said the righteous Judge to His rebellious creature, till then incorruptible and immortal, "and to dust thou shalt return." (WJW, vol. 7, 346)

The Power Behind the Apostles' Ministry (2 Cor. 4:7–15)

Paul next contrasted the weakness of all human messengers with the power of God, who enables them. **We have this treasure in jars of clay** (v. 7). The **treasure** was the gospel ("the light of the knowledge of the glory of God in the face of Christ"). The **jars of clay** were the human bearers of the good news. The clay lamps and pots that contained burning oil that provided light were fragile and inexpensive. Yet they were used to hold treasures. In triumphal processions, conquerors would display captured treasures in clay pots. Some have referred to the jars of clay as throwaway containers and suggested that Paul today might have referred to paper plates. The **treasure** was **in** the **jars of clay to show that this all-surpassing power is from God and not from** the human messengers (v. 7).

Paul said although he was **hard pressed on every side** (v. 8), he never found himself cornered without escape. Although he experienced perplexity, he never was utterly at a loss. Although he suffered persecution, he was never left by himself. Although he had endured knockdowns, he was never put out of action by a knockout. While the apostles carried **around** in their bodies **the death of Jesus**, it was **so that the life of Jesus may also be revealed** (v. 10). The apostles' ministry was going to lead to their deaths, and they were committed to serve Jesus even to the death. It is true of every follower of Jesus that they must be willing to take up their cross and follow Him even if it means death. But at the same time, the resurrected life of Jesus **is at work** in us (v. 12).

WORDS FROM WESLEY

2 Corinthians 4:10

Always—Wherever we go, *bearing about in the body the dying of the Lord Jesus*—Continually expecting to lay down our lives like Him; *that the life also of Jesus might be manifested in our body*—That we may also rise and be glorified like Him. (ENNT)

Paul quoted Psalm 116:10 and declared that it was on the basis of his faith he spoke the Lord's message. It was **because we know that the one who raised the Lord Jesus from the dead will also raise us with Jesus** (2 Cor. 4:14). He didn't leave out his readers—**and present us with you in his presence** (v. 14). The power of God through Jesus' resurrected life, appropriated by faith, made it possible for the disciples and us to triumph over all difficulties.

Paul made it clear God's purposes included his readers—**All this is for your benefit** (v. 15). Then he made an optimistic statement that reverberated with confidence and triumph—**so that the grace that is reaching more and more people may cause thanksgiving to overflow to the glory of God** (v. 15). In the face of all Paul's trials and tribulations, his cause was advancing and multitudes were being brought to the Lord. For the same reasons it can be so for us.

WORDS FROM WESLEY

2 Corinthians 4:15

For all things—Whether adverse or prosperous, *are for your sakes*—For the profit of all that believe, as well as all that preach, *that the overflowing grace*—Which continues you alive both in soul and body, might abound yet more *through the thanksgiving of many*—For thanksgiving invites more abundant grace. (ENNT)

The Eternal Glory Resulting from the Apostles' Ministry (2 Cor. 4:16–18)

On the basis of God's power, appropriated by faith, Paul did **not lose heart** (v. 16). While his body was **outwardly . . . wasting away** (aging, weakening), **inwardly** (spiritually) he was **being renewed day by day** (v. 16). He made an amazing contrast. On the one side, he put the hard-pressed, perplexed, persecuted, and struck-down experiences. Then, on the other side, he characterized them all as **light and momentary troubles** (v. 17). These were **achieving for** him **an eternal glory that far outweighs them all** (v. 17). It is difficult to get the full effect of the Greek for this verse. The Greek word used in 4:7 for "all-surpassing" is doubled here in 4:17, used twice to try to picture how much the eternal glory outweighs the light and momentary troubles.

The Greek word for **glory** translates a Hebrew word derived from a concept of weight. So superlative is piled on top of superlative to make the contrast as extreme as words can make it. In essence, afflictions here will not even be remembered when eternal glory is ours. Thus, Paul declared, **So we fix our eyes not on what is seen, but on what is unseen. For what is seen is temporary, but what is unseen is eternal** (v. 18).

DISCUSSION

Is humility a rare quality today in a culture that encourages self-esteem and self-acclaim? How different Paul's attitude was. He perceived himself and his fellow workers as simply clay vessels in whom God had placed a priceless treasure—the gospel.

1. How might a church of immature Christians impede the progress of the gospel?

2. Why is it humbling to know God has committed the gospel message to you?

3. What keeps you faithful to God when trials come upon you?

4. Why do you agree or disagree that it is possible to proclaim the gospel with wrong motives?

5. What should motivate Christians to proclaim the gospel?

6. Read 2 Corinthians 4:4. What philosophies or ideas do you think Satan uses today to blind the lost to the gospel?

7. Read 2 Corinthians 4:16–18. How have you been "renewed day by day"?

8. Why do you agree or disagree that the best things in life are not things?

PRAYER

God, show us opportunities to point out how strong You are, especially when we appear to be weak.

11

CHRIST'S AMBASSADORS

2 Corinthians 5:11—6:2

———————

Believers in Jesus Christ naturally become ambassadors for Him.

Serving as an ambassador to a foreign country doesn't always involve living in luxurious surroundings and attending lavish state dinners. Sometimes an ambassador finds him- or herself in a hostile environment. But a faithful ambassador endeavors to bridge the culture gap, demonstrate genuine friendship for the people to whom he or she has been sent, and try to represent his or her own country admirably.

Christopher Stevens, US Ambassador to Libya, loved and served the Libyan people. However, on September 11, 2012, terrorists brutally murdered him and three other Americans.

This study tells what it means to be ambassadors for Christ. Who is willing to do whatever this high honor demands?

COMMENTARY

The context of Paul's second letter to the Corinthians is reconciliation through forgiveness. He wrote, "If anyone has caused grief . . . the punishment inflicted on him by the majority is sufficient for him. Now instead, you ought to forgive him and comfort him, so that he will not be overwhelmed by excessive sorrow. I urge you, therefore, to reaffirm your love for him" (2 Cor. 2:5–8). This man may be the same one Paul told the Corinthians to expel in his first letter (1 Cor. 5:1–2). The difference in this letter is due to the repentance of the Corinthians in response to his first letter (2 Cor. 7:8–16).

In the first letter, Paul dealt severely with divisions in the church (1 Cor. 1:10–12). His resolution for them was for the Corinthians to imitate him (4:16). To this end, Paul sent Timothy to remind them of Paul's way of life in Christ Jesus (4:17). The idea is that Paul's way of life in Christ Jesus was distinct from the way of life that is worldly. Today we call this distinction *perspective* or *worldview*. We use these words to describe the way different people see the world and other people with whom they interact. Another word we use for this is *ideology*. What does our ideal world look like? How does it function? These questions go beyond sensory perceptions (what we see, hear, taste, touch, and smell).

What we see with our eyes and hear with our ears have powerful effects on our minds. At one point, Paul told the Corinthians they were looking only on the surface of things (2 Cor. 10:7). If we fall into this trap, then we may lament, "The LORD has forsaken me, the Lord has forgotten me" (Isa. 49:14). However, if we adopt Paul's way of life in Christ Jesus, we will hear the Lord say to us, "Can a mother forget the baby at her breast and have no compassion on the child she has borne? Though she may forget, I will not forget you!" (Isa. 49:15).

The way of life in this world is ruled by passions—lust, greed, jealousy, anger, ambition, and the like. The way of life in Christ Jesus is ruled by God's passion to reconcile all people to himself. These are constructed by opposing worldviews. We must look on the world we can see with a wary eye, for all is not as it seems. We must look upon the world we cannot see with constant faith. "For just as the sufferings of Christ flow over into our lives, so also through Christ our comfort overflows" (2 Cor.1:5). "So we fix our eyes not on what is seen, but on what is unseen. For what is seen is temporary, but what is unseen is eternal" (2 Cor. 4:18).

The Fear of the Lord Is the Beginning (2 Cor. 5:11)

The phrase "the fear of the Lord" occurs once in Job, three times in the Psalms, and eleven times in Proverbs. These Scriptures might have influenced Paul's use of **fear of the Lord** in 2 Corinthians 5:11. While it is impossible to determine if he had a specific verse in mind, two of them provide an interesting backdrop for the content of the letter in general and the passage at hand.

Proverbs 15:16 says, "Better a little with the fear of the Lord than great wealth with turmoil." In 2 Corinthians 1:8–11, Paul spoke of the great hardships they faced in Asia and said, "But this happened that we might not rely on ourselves but on God, who raises the dead" (v. 9). Then in 4:17, he wrote, "For our light and momentary troubles are achieving for us an eternal glory that far outweighs them all" (compare Rom. 8:18). Most directly, Paul used his hardships in chapter 11 as credentials for authority in the church. If external hardships were not enough, Paul added his daily concern for the people to the list. "Who is weak, and I do not feel weak? Who is led into sin, and I do not inwardly burn?" (2 Cor. 11:29). Thus, Paul established throughout the letter that he had little in the way of the life of this world. What he did have of it was trouble. Instead, he sought to increase his understanding of the fear of the Lord, since "the fear of the Lord leads to life: Then one rests content, untouched by trouble" (Prov. 19:23).

Psalm 34:11 says, "Come, my children, listen to me; I will teach you the fear of the Lord." In 1 Corinthians 4:15 and 2 Corinthians 12:14–15, Paul framed his relationship with the Corinthians as a father and his children. This relationship was not confined to the Corinthians, but to anyone who came to the Lord through Paul's ministry. It was his own fear of the Lord that equipped him to lead other souls into the kingdom of life. Paul and his companions tried to persuade people to have faith in the gospel because they could. However, this ability gave them a responsibility—an obligation.

The Clarity of Nonsense and the Nonsense of Clarity (2 Cor. 5:11–15)

In these verses, Paul helped the church reestablish a correct worldview. He began with the statement, **What we are is plain to God** (v. 11), thus establishing his clear conscience toward people, since he was under the judgment of God (see also 1 Cor. 4:4). Because God knew his heart, he did not bear the burden of convincing others of his sincerity. That is how Paul could say he was not trying to convince them even though he was using persuasive and passionate language.

WORDS FROM WESLEY
2 Corinthians 5:14

For the love of Christ to us, and our love to Him, constraineth us—Both to the one and the other, beareth us on with such a strong, steady, prevailing influence, as winds and tides exert when they waft the vessel to its destined harbour; *while we thus judge, that if Christ died for all, then were all*, even the best of men, naturally *dead*—In a state of spiritual death, and liable to death eternal. For had any man been otherwise, Christ had not needed to have died for him. (ENNT)

Here is a crucial point in the Christian worldview: Even though we do not have responsibility for the outcome, we are obligated to spread the gospel passionately and by all means at our disposal. Two things come from this approach. First, those whom we affect can have confidence in us, especially when others try to discredit us in the eyes of people we are trying to reach. This happened to Paul. People came to the Lord under his ministry, and others tried to discredit him so the people who trusted him would become suspicious. The same is true today. When people are saved, their friends and family will accuse the church of (among other things) brainwashing them to steal their money. While we do not have to prove ourselves to anyone, if we live openly and honestly, those who trust us will have reason to continue in the face of **those who take pride in what is seen rather than what is in the heart** (v. 12).

Second, if we are passionate about and diligent in the honest and open work of the gospel, any radicalism will be dismissed as eccentricity. So, **if we are out of our mind, it is for the sake of God; if we are in our right mind, it is for** those to whom we are serving the gospel (v. 13). Again, "Through love and faithfulness sin is atoned for; through the fear of the LORD a man avoids evil" (Prov. 16:6). Openness before others is not a tool to convince them of our trustworthiness, but a tool to defeat the Enemy's attempts to discourage them. So when Satan raises doubts in their minds concerning the integrity of their Christian friends, they can brush them aside as matters for God, and focus instead on the basic facts of the gospel—**because we are convinced that one died for all, and therefore all died . . . that those who live should no longer live for themselves but for him who died for them** (2 Cor. 5:14–15).

WORDS FROM WESLEY

2 Corinthians 5:15

And that he died for all—That all might be saved, *that they who live*—That all who live upon the earth, *should not henceforth*—From the moment they know Him, *live unto themselves*—Seek their own honour, profit, pleasure, *but unto him*—In all righteousness and true holiness. (ENNT)

Jesus: The Cosmic Axis (2 Cor. 5:16–19)

According to Paul, how you view the world is determined by how you view Christ. If you view Jesus as the One who died and was raised again, you cannot view anything the same way you did before. This view of Christ is the line of demarcation between what is *worldly* and what is *godly*. Because the resurrection of Jesus throws all life and creation into a new light, **anyone . . . in Christ** (v. 17) must be viewed in the light of the resurrection. That is, we cannot be viewed from a vantage that defines us in terms of intellectual, physical, emotional, or financial status. Our worth is located in our hearts and in the heart of God.

WORDS FROM WESLEY

2 Corinthians 5:17

Therefore if any one be in Christ—A true believer in Him, *there is a new creation*—Only the power that makes a world, can make a Christian. And when he is so created, *the old things are passed away*—Of their own accord, even as snow in spring. Behold! the present, visible, undeniable change! *All things are become new*—He has new life, new senses, new faculties, new affections, new appetites, new ideas and conceptions. His whole tenor of action and conversation is new, and he lives, as it were, in a new world. God, men, the whole creation, heaven, earth, and all therein, appear in a new light, and stand related to him in a new manner, since he was created anew in Christ Jesus. (ENNT)

The heart of God is to forgive and effect reconciliation. The heart of the world is to seek retribution. In the crucifixion, these two worldviews collided. In the resurrection, God's view was eternally revealed. That revelation included the reconciliation of the *entire* world, **not counting men's sins against them** (v. 19). As Paul said of himself, "My conscience is clear, but that does not make me innocent" (1 Cor. 4:4). God forgives the guilty and reconciles the exiled, not because they are any less guilty, but because God is surpassingly gracious.

"Let the wicked forsake his way and the evil man his thoughts. Let him turn to the LORD, and he will have mercy on him, and to our God, for he will freely pardon. 'For my thoughts are not your thoughts, neither are your ways my ways,' declares the LORD" (Isa. 55:7–8). "Godly sorrow brings repentance that leads to salvation . . . but worldly sorrow brings death" (2 Cor. 7:10). **So from now on we regard no one from a worldly point of view** (5:16).

The Time Has Come (2 Cor. 5:19—6:2)

Augustine called Isaiah "the fifth gospel." It seems prophecy was the backdrop for much of Paul's thought. Here he addressed Isaiah 49:8 with the same sense Jesus introduced Isaiah 61:1–2 in Luke 4:18–19. In Luke's record, after Jesus read the words of the prophet, He said, "Today this scripture is fulfilled in your hearing" (Luke 4:21). In 2 Corinthians, Paul said the same thing about Isaiah 49:8—**I tell you, now is the time of God's favor, now is the day of salvation** (2 Cor. 6:2).

WORDS FROM WESLEY

2 Corinthians 5:20

What unparalleled condescension and divinely tender mercies are displayed in this verse? Did the judge ever beseech a condemned criminal to accept of pardon? Does the creditor ever beseech a ruined debtor to receive an acquittance in full? Yet our Almighty Lord, and our eternal Judge, not only vouchsafes to offer these blessings, but invites us, entreats us, and with the moat tender importunity, solicits us, not to reject them. (ENNT)

The repetition of **now** compounded with the urgency of Paul's language in general (for example, **We implore you on Christ's behalf** [5:20]) necessitates that we emphasize *now*. After all the arguments have been made, after the case has been borne out, what was promised in Isaiah has been fulfilled in Jesus. We must *now* "seek the LORD while he may be found" and "call on him while he is near" (Isa. 55:6). For "from now on [He] will tell [us] of new things, of hidden things unknown to [us]" (Isa. 48:6).

It is this revelation of unknown things that has been made known in Jesus. God destroyed death. If death is humanity's greatest fear, how much should we fear the One who defeated death? Though the fear of the Lord should be exponentially greater than the fear of death, it is a different type of fear. The fear of death is the fear of destruction. "The fear of the LORD is a fountain of life, turning a man from the snares of death" (Prov. 14:27).

It was the deep personal experience of Paul and his coworkers that compelled them to preach the message of reconciliation. God committed this message to them. He bound it to them through the same grace and forgiveness with which He refused to count their sins against them. Instead, God made Paul, and all who believe, His **fellow workers** (2 Cor. 6:1) to be an example and model of a new worldview that sees the world through the lens of heaven instead of the eyes of human beings.

WORDS FROM WESLEY

2 Corinthians 5:21

He made him a sin-offering, who knew no sin—A commendation peculiar to Christ: *for us*—Who knew no righteousness, who were inwardly and outwardly nothing but sin, who must have been consumed by the divine justice, had not this atonement been made for our sins, *that we might be made the righteous people of God through him*—Might through Him be invested with that righteousness, first imputed to us, then implanted in us, which is in every sense the righteousness of God. (ENNT)

DISCUSSION

Do you agree that an ambassador should be persuasive? Discuss if he or she should try to reconcile his or her country and the country to which he or she was sent. Discuss if his or her love for the sending country should compel the ambassador to carry out his or her mission zealously.

1. How has your fear of the Lord strengthened your walk with the Lord? Your service for the Lord?

2. Why do you agree or disagree that it doesn't matter what unbelievers think of Christians?

3. Why do you agree or disagree that many unbelievers do not understand such terms as *salvation, born again,* and *grace?*

4. How would you explain the way of salvation in terms most unbelievers would understand?

5. How would you respond if someone charged that TV preachers are only interested in money?

6. How does the teaching given in 2 Corinthians 5:15 relate to the life of an ambassador of Christ?

7. Read 2 Corinthians 5:17. What major changes have you experienced since you became a Christian?

8. Why do you agree or disagree that serving as an ambassador for Christ is life's greatest privilege?

PRAYER

What a privilege it is to be Your ambassadors to people in need of You, Lord God! Please give us Your insight to represent You in ways that help reconcile each one to You.

12

GRACE-FILLED GENEROSITY

2 Corinthians 8:6–15; 9:6–15

Obedience to the gospel of Christ compels us to cheerful generosity.

An entrepreneur vowed to tithe the profits from his start-up company if God would make it successful. As the company grew, the businessman kept his promise. However, when the company became hugely successful, the tithe seemed too large to give to God. So the businessman asked his pastor to pray that God would release him from his vow.

"I can't do that," the pastor replied, "but I can ask God to reduce your company to its original size so you will find the smaller tithe much easier to give."

This study highlights the fact that God loves a cheerful giver, and it teaches us to give cheerfully and generously to Him.

COMMENTARY

Paul wrote 2 Corinthians to celebrate reconciliation within the Corinthian church and between a rebellious portion of that church and himself. What caused this dispute, the settlement of which caused Paul such joy? One or more pompous church members in Corinth had sought to undermine Paul's ministry.

In Acts 18:1–18, Luke narrated Paul's first visit to Corinth, a fruitful eighteen-month encounter that enabled Paul to share the good news of Jesus in this city and disciple many believers. How did the church fare after Paul's departure? There was good news and bad news.

The good news was that many people in the church continued to grow in grace and knowledge. These had a few questions and sent word to Paul (at the time planting churches around Ephesus) for answers. At the same time, Paul received word that a few local Christians were behaving badly (see 1 Cor. 6), in a manner that damaged the reputation of the church. Paul responded with what we know as 1 Corinthians. Within that letter, he answered the questions and strongly corrected those who had fallen into a sinful lifestyle.

Many Corinthian Christians received Paul's instructions with gratitude, but a few moved into full-scale rebellion. In response to this life-threatening division within the Corinthian church, Paul made a difficult (and likely short) trip to Corinth and wrote an equally painful letter that apparently has not survived.

From Ephesus Paul sent Titus to Corinth with the anguished letter. Then Paul waited. Titus had promised he would return to Paul via a land route. After Paul had waited as long as he could, he started out for Corinth, hoping to meet Titus along the way. He traveled first to Troas, but did not find Titus there (2:12). Continuing around the Aegean Sea, Paul came next to Macedonia (perhaps Philippi). There Paul did find Titus, who brought wonderful news: All believers in Corinth were ready to come again under the loving arm of their spiritual father Paul (7:5–7).

Paul felt such relief that right there he wrote the letter we call 2 Corinthians. Paul devoted most of this letter to explaining his recent thoughts and feelings, as well as offering a more complete picture of his ministry, seeking to eliminate any confusion and misunderstanding remaining in the Corinthian church. Paul again used Titus as the mailman. This time, however, Titus did not travel alone. A group of Christians from several communities accompanied him (8:16–17, 22–24; Acts 20:4 lists men who may have been part of this traveling party). Why? We find the answer to that question in 2 Corinthians 8 and 9.

Throughout these chapters, Paul's words revolved around an offering he was collecting. Before reviewing elements of Paul's thinking about the Corinthians' participation in the offering, we should look at the offering and its purpose. The church in Jerusalem was facing hard times. Years earlier, when Jerusalem had faced a food shortage, the Antioch church had sent money to help meet that need. (Paul had helped carry this contribution from Antioch to Jerusalem; Acts 11:27–30.) At this point during Paul's third missionary journey, Jerusalem again experienced a need.

In a gesture that would help the receiving Christians in Jerusalem and the giving Christians across the northern Mediterranean region, Paul organized a multi-church collection. Paul hoped both to help feed hungry Christians in Jerusalem and to strengthen relationships among Jewish and Gentile Christians.

Paul's Encouragement to Give (2 Cor. 8:6–15)

Paul used at least five thoughts to motivate the Corinthians to give generously.

He began his motivational speech in the opening verses of 2 Corinthians 8. There, Paul first motivated the church in Corinth by employing a bit of friendly competition (see vv. 1–7). In this spirit of informal contest, Paul could avoid using his apostolic authority (**I am not commanding you**; v. 8), since some of his previous strong instructions had led to a rebellion within the Corinthian church.

Paul, taking his readers back to the treatise on love in 1 Corinthians 13, wrote, **I want to test the sincerity of your love** (2 Cor. 8:8). He anticipated the Corinthian Christians would demonstrate true love—not merely in words, but in financial sacrifice. The Macedonians had emptied their pockets, even when their bank accounts were low. If Christians to the north could do that, the wealthier Corinthians could give the same or more.

Paul continued his pep talk with a more foundational comparison. **Though** Christ **was rich, yet for your sakes he became poor, so that you through his poverty might become rich** (v. 9). Compare Paul's words in another context: Christ "did not consider equality with God something to be grasped, but made himself nothing" (Phil. 2:6–7). If Jesus laid down His physical life (John 10:18; Rom. 8:32) so the Corinthians could enjoy spiritual life, how much more could they open their wallets so other Christians could continue in joyful service to the Savior?

WORDS FROM WESLEY
2 Corinthians 8:9

For ye know—And this knowledge is the true source of love, *the grace*—The most sincere, most free, and most abundant love. *He became poor*—In becoming man, in all His life; in His death: *rich*—In the favour and image of God. (ENNT)

Next, the apostle praised the Corinthians' track record (see 2 Cor. 8:10–11, compare v. 6). Paul had, a few verses earlier, patted this church on the back: **Just as you excel in everything—in faith, in speech, in knowledge, in complete earnestness and in your love for us—see that you also excel in this grace of giving** (v. 7). Were these words flattery? With the trauma some Corinthians had forced on Paul, you might think so. At the same time, no doubt many had followed Paul in following Jesus.

Paul moved next to a comparison between fine thinking and concrete action. In verses 11–12, Paul echoed words the apostle James wrote: "Suppose a brother or sister is without clothes and daily food. If one of you says to him, 'Go, I wish you well; keep warm and well fed,' but does nothing about his physical needs, what good is it?" (James 2:15–16). Deciding is not acting. The

Corinthians had promised to give. Here Paul called them to follow through.

The fifth motivating factor Paul used was a hint about the future (2 Cor. 8:13–15). The Lord said it best: "Give, and it will be given to you. A good measure, pressed down, shaken together and running over, will be poured into your lap. For with the measure you use, it will be measured to you" (Luke 6:38). Paul reminded the Corinthians the situations of Jerusalem and Corinth might someday be reversed. If the Corinthians gave at the time of Jerusalem's need, perhaps Jerusalem or some other group of churches would later relieve a Corinthian period of poverty.

●

WORDS FROM WESLEY

2 Corinthians 8:14

As the temporal bounty of the Corinthians did now supply the temporal wants of their poor brethren in Judea; so the prayers of these might be a means of bringing down many spiritual blessings on their benefactors. So that all the spiritual wants of the one might be amply supplied; all the temporal of the other. (ENNT)

Paul's Promises for Generous Givers (2 Cor. 9:6–11)

In the statement that opens this block from Paul's letter, he took a soft hint from the previous section and restated it as a firm promise. The hint: "If you give to others now, someone else might later give to you." The promise: **Whoever sows sparingly will also reap sparingly, and whoever sows generously will also reap generously** (v. 6). Is this a promise that if the Corinthians together gave one talent of gold, God would reward them with an unexpected windfall of three talents? No, neither they nor we can manipulate God in this manner. Yet, all other things being equal, the farmer who sows ten acres will receive twice as much of the same crop as the farmer who sows five acres.

God's economy works on a different plan. When we give generously to God and others, God will not ignore our bigheartedness. God may not reward money with money, chicken soup with chicken soup, but He never fails to reward those who give—with joy, friendship, or sometimes a larger bowl of chicken soup. Paul encouraged the Corinthians to watch, not *if* but *how* God would minister to them for their giving to others.

Perhaps God's reward would be the gift of **righteousness** (v. 10). Salvation by works? Never. True righteousness always involves far more than earning points with God. True righteousness is the gift of a right relationship (a God-prepared relationship) with God and with people.

What kind of givers please God most? Which givers does God most cheerfully reward? Those who have given cheerfully. (The Greek word behind **cheerful** [v. 7] comes from the same root as the English word *hilarious*.) Picture two gifts. One comes from a group motivated by guilt. The other comes from people who give with such joy that they are overcome with laughter. The recipient may buy the same amount of food with either gift, but which giver gains more? For our own good, God wants us to give as freely as He gave to us.

Does God reward cheerful givers? Of course. He blesses them after they give, but Christians can receive as grace from God even the opportunity to give. God never promised any Christian would have financial wealth to share, but God never leaves any person without something (a gift of time, encouragement, self) to give. Yes, **God is able to make all grace abound to you, so that in all things at all times, having all that you need, you will abound in every good work** (v. 8). Even the poor receive and can share God's bounty—in some form. God is faithful to all His people (v. 9, quoting Ps. 112:9).

●

WORDS FROM WESLEY

2 Corinthians 9:8

All grace—Every kind of blessing, *that ye may abound to every good work*—God gives us every thing, that we may do good therewith, and so receive more blessings. All things in this life, even rewards, are, to the faithful, seeds in order to a future harvest. (ENNT)

Do generous people end up rich? Perhaps. But better yet, God rewards His people in multiple ways, so they have multiple gifts to offer others (v. 11). Recipients of God's varied generosity glory not only in the gift, not only in human givers, but may find, through receiving, the identity of the ultimate Giver, thanking Him and being moved toward their own renewed relationships with Him.

Paul's Thanksgiving for God's Gift of Community (2 Cor. 9:12–15)

In the last words of verse 11, Paul moved from promising rewards for generosity to expressing gratitude for the privilege he and all God's people share as part of a community of generosity. With this line of thinking, Paul finished the segment of 2 Corinthians he devoted to the offering for Jerusalem. **This service that you perform is not only supplying the needs of God's people but is also overflowing in many expressions of thanks to God** (v. 12). In other words, "What you are doing for Jerusalem is wonderful, but you are serving Christians everywhere by showing how much you care."

When your church helps feed hungry people, you receive the joy of giving. The hungry are glad to eat. And, though good press should not be your primary motivation, others in your community—both Christians and non-Christians—will be moved to gratitude and potential action by reports of your church's love in action. People **will praise God for the obedience that accompanies your confession of the gospel of Christ** (v. 13). **Thanks be to God for his indescribable gift!** (v. 15). The gift of salvation? Of course. But in the context of Paul's original writing, "Thank You, God, for the gift of Christian community!" Let's join Paul in celebrating the great family God has given us. And let's keep reaching out in practical ways to others who know Jesus and those who could join God's wonderful community.

WORDS FROM WESLEY
2 Corinthians 9:15

His unspeakable gift—His outward and inward blessings, the number and excellence of which cannot be uttered. (ENNT)

DISCUSSION

To what extent does a holy life include generosity? Discuss if a person is holy if he or she withholds money from God.

1. Do you agree or disagree that the New Testament commands believers to tithe?

2. Do you think Christians should give at least a tenth of their income to the Lord's work? Why or why not?

3. How might generosity manifest itself beyond financial giving?

4. Read 2 Corinthians 8:7. Why is generous giving called a grace?

5. How did Jesus' "generosity" make you rich?

6. Why do you agree or disagree that believers should not give in order to gain something from God in return?

7. Should Christians give to the relief of needy people in your community or should the relief be limited to needy Christians? Defend your answer.

8. How has generous giving brought personal joy to you?

9. Should a believer not give at all if he or she can't give joyfully? Why or why not?

PRAYER

God, You have been so generous to us—especially through the gift of Your Son. Help us reflect Your remarkable generosity to others this week.

13

DRAWING ON HIS STRENGTH

2 Corinthians 11:30—12:10

God reveals His power through our weaknesses.

The words *boast* and *boost* differ by only one letter. Perhaps the similarity is significant because usually a person boasts because he or she hopes to boost his or her reputation.

One day, as King Nebuchadnezzar was walking on the roof of his palace, he boasted about his accomplishments. He bragged that he had built everything by his mighty power and for the glory of his majesty (Dan. 4:30). But God answered the king's boasting by sentencing him to seven years of living like an animal away from people. The sentence would end only when Nebuchadnezzar learned that God is sovereign.

Ego-based boasting is always wrong, but as this study shows, boasting that glorifies the Lord is commendable.

COMMENTARY

After devoting chapters 8 and 9 of 2 Corinthians to the offering for Christians in Jerusalem, Paul returned to the letter's broader theme: the settling of a recent dispute among Corinthian Christians and between some Corinthian church members and Paul. Second Corinthians 10 and 11 hint at Paul's feelings of uncertainty. Although Titus had brought Paul good news of reconciliation, Paul still feared his relationship with the rebellious Corinthians, as well as those they had influenced, might need further healing.

Some in Corinth felt their credentials and authority surpassed anything on Paul's résumé. Paul saw himself as an apostle of Jesus

Christ. These competitors saw themselves as "super-apostles" (11:5). As these "false apostles" (11:13) had boasted over evidence for their supposed position, Paul responded by his own boasting. In contrast to the Corinthian leaders, Paul boasted less of his pedigree (11:21–23) than of the pain he had endured (11:23–29). Rather than pointing at his abilities, Paul highlighted his weaknesses and God's superior strength and grace (11:30—12:10).

Boasting about God's Gift of Life (2 Cor. 11:30–33)

Boasting is a primary theme of 2 Corinthians 10 and 11. Paul felt a need to boast before the Corinthians only because false apostles had asserted the superiority of themselves and their message over anything Paul was or had said. (Even then, Paul boasted not to prove he was right, but for the benefit of the Corinthian Christians who were being swayed from Jesus Christ.)

Paul preferred not to boast. In fact, as he opened his Corinthian correspondence, Paul had described the humility with which he had approached the people of Corinth (see 1 Cor. 2:1–5). But when Christians in this city took advantage of Paul's modesty, he moved out of his preferred mode toward self-defense. **If I must boast, I will boast of the things that show my weakness** (2 Cor. 11:30).

Paul listed many persecutions he had endured (11:23–29). Obviously he had survived each of these horrors; otherwise he could not have described his pain. In 11:30—12:10, Paul highlighted deliverance from one disaster: being lowered over the city wall in Damascus. Out of all the examples Paul had given earlier in the chapter, why did Paul pick this one? Paul chose the first time he had been persecuted as a Christian.

Acts 9 opened with Paul (then known as Saul) on his way to Damascus (the central city of Syria) to arrest Christians in that city. But, as Saul neared Damascus, God intervened. God spoke both to Saul and to Ananias, a Damascus church member. God brought these men together and in the process turned Saul around. The great persecutor became one of the persecuted. As Saul proclaimed Jesus in Damascus, Jews became jealous and sought his arrest. They connived with the local governor, who served under the pagan king of the region: Aretas. (Aretas was father-in-law to Herod Antipas, the Herod who interacted with Jesus and John the Baptist.) Assuming Saul would leave Damascus in the customary manner, guards were assigned to watch the city gate. Under cover of darkness, friends placed Saul in a basket and roped their cargo over the city wall (Acts 9:22–25).

Why did Paul highlight this first time he suffered persecution for Jesus? First, Paul was praising God (**the God and Father of the Lord Jesus Christ, who is to be praised forever** [2 Cor. 11:31]) and not his own ability. Second, Paul could remind the Corinthians of his seniority in the faith. Contrasted with Christians in Corinth, many of whom Paul had led to Jesus, Paul had lived in relationship with Jesus fifteen years longer than any supposed "super-apostle." Third, without directly describing how God had uniquely interacted with Paul (on the road to Damascus), Paul could remind his readers of this unique event.

Boasting about God's Gift of a Vision (2 Cor. 12:1–6)

After boasting of God dramatically protecting him, Paul shifted his bragging toward another act of God: the gift of a dramatic vision. Paul, attempting to keep his focus on God and not himself, described himself in the third person. Instead of straightforwardly saying God enabled him to see heaven, Paul spoke of **a man** or **this man** (vv. 2–3). At the same time, this experience fits in this large block of evidence only if God lifted Paul himself **to the third heaven** (v. 2).

Why did Paul use this thinly veiled attempt to hide his identity? Paul evidently felt he needed to tell this story, undoubtedly one of the highlights of his life. At the same time, he used the strategy of third-person language, attempting to reduce the chances his readers would see his narrative as nothing but perverse pride.

Along with describing himself obliquely, Paul used negative hyperbole to introduce the story in verse 1: **Although there is nothing to be gained, I** tell you this story. If Paul had seen no value in writing verses 1–5, he would not have included this account. He did see something to be gained, but wanted, in one sense, to downplay the significance of this life experience.

For the Corinthians, Paul dated this vision. Evidence informs scholars that he wrote this letter in roughly A.D. 55. So, **fourteen years** (v. 2) prior would place Paul somewhere near Tarsus in a period of his ministry otherwise unknown to us. (See Acts 9:30.) Where did the vision take Paul? Into **the third heaven** (v. 2). Within the ancient worldview, the first heaven would indicate the visible sky. A second level of heaven would indicate the region of the sun and other heavenly bodies. If Paul entered **the third heaven**, he came into the presence of God. (For other references to multiple layers of heavens, verses describing Jesus traveling through the heavens, see Heb. 4:14; 7:26; and Eph. 4:10.) Paul placed his vision in **paradise** (2 Cor. 12:4), another New Testament description of God's dwelling (Luke 23:43; Phil. 1:23; and 2 Cor. 5:8).

WORDS FROM WESLEY

2 Corinthians 12:2

The third heaven—Where God is; far above the aerial and the starry heaven. Some suppose it was here the apostle was let into the mystery of the future state of the church: and received his orders to turn from the Jews and go to the Gentiles. (ENNT)

Paul knew his experience was real. At the same time, the apostle did not know precisely how the vision appeared to him, whether God literally lifted him through the heavens or if, in his mind, God unveiled this panorama. Again, perhaps to prevent an appearance of pride, Paul twice admitted a degree of uncertainty in relation to this supernatural event (vv. 2–3).

What did Paul sense while in the third heaven? Perhaps because God had forbidden Paul to describe God's home, or again to offer an attitude of humility (or perhaps both), Paul offered no details of what he saw and heard (v. 4). Nowhere in Scripture does any writer picture heaven in detail. We read only analogies that give delightful hints.

God had given Paul this revelation not because Paul deserved it. If he had merited such splendor, Paul could brag about his qualifications. No, Paul preferred to tell this story as if God had chosen him at random. Who experienced heaven? "Well," Paul would have to say, "I did, but as I look back, I realize I was hardly any more than 'that man,' some anonymous person."

Could Paul have legitimately boasted? Briefly he admitted that he could have done so. (At that moment, Paul may have been thinking back to material he included in 11:21–23.) Although he could have challenged the Corinthian "super-apostles" to a divine contest and easily defeated them (following the pattern of Elijah's competition with the prophets of Baal [1 Kings 18:16–46]), Paul focused his boasting on God, rather than on himself (2 Cor. 12:6).

WORDS FROM WESLEY

2 Corinthians 12:6

But I forbear—I speak sparingly of these things, for fear any one should think too highly *of me*—O where is this fear now to be found? Who is afraid of this? (ENNT)

Boasting About God's Gift of a Thorn (2 Cor. 12:7–10)

As Paul moved toward bragging over his weakness, in an aside, he admitted that the man of 12:1–6 was himself: "God gave **me . . . these surpassingly great revelations**" (v. 7; Paul seemed to have hinted that he had seen God and heaven more than once). "The same God, however, wanted to keep me humble. To accomplish that goal, God allowed me the trauma of **a thorn in my flesh**" (v. 7).

WORDS FROM WESLEY

2 Corinthians 12:7

Saviour, to Thee for help I sue,
O bring Thy tempted servant through
The danger and distress;
Thrust out, destroy the inbred fiend,
And bid my bosom-conflict end
In never-ending peace.
Still in mine agony I pray,
Take, Jesus, take this thorn away,
Command him to depart
This cruel messenger of hell,
And O, for ever, Lord, expel
His nature from my heart.
Sore buffeted, I ask again
Deliverance from my sin and pain;
Thou hear'st my bitterest cry:
Tempted above what I can bear,
O might I now escape the snare,
And bless my God, and die! (PW, vol. 13, 55–56)

Scholars and lay Bible readers have puzzled for centuries, trying to discern the character of Paul's thorn. Possibilities include persecution (see v. 10) and temptation (either sexual or spiritual, such as, a desire for a softer life). A majority of scholars opt for some type of physical discomfort, anything from an ugly appearance (see v. 10), epilepsy, severe headaches, or eye problems. Galatians 6:11 hints at poor eyesight, infections, or malaria. (Paul suffered from some illness when he first visited Galatia [4:13–14].)

Paul used the word **thorn** as an analogy. Had his problem been a literal thorn, doctor Luke would have most likely removed it. A thorn in Paul's flesh seems to point toward physical pain. Paul's condition tormented him (2 Cor. 12:7). From this many have argued Paul's problem was an intermittent one. Within this possibility, on most days, Paul could carry out his ministry, but occasionally, the pain knocked him flat.

What insights can we gain from **messenger of Satan** (v. 7)? Paul did not directly blame God for his discomfort. The immediate cause was Satan, the spiritual Enemy. At the same time, the sovereign God rules Satan. Satan can do no more than God allows. Also, when Paul asked for the thorn to be taken from him, he made his request, not to Satan, but to **the Lord** (v. 8).

Whatever condition Paul illustrated with the word **thorn**, Paul could boast in the problems it caused him. The Lord gave Paul two assurances: the thorn fit into God's plan, and the thorn would not overwhelm Paul. **"My grace is sufficient for you, for my power is made perfect in weakness"** (v. 9).

At this point, Paul felt no need to hide his identity. Many readers might envy a heavenly experience. None of them would seek to share Paul's pain. All but the most stubborn would recognize that Paul here praised God alone. Only God in His grace and strength could enable Paul to live with a deadly disablement.

Because of its helpful side effects, Paul could even delight in his weaknesses, knowing they reminded him of God's sufficiency. Paul rejoiced that God's power rested upon him (v. 9). When Paul depended on his own traits or abilities (v. 6), he would fail. Yet, in relying on God's power, he always succeeded, not for his own glory, but **for Christ's sake** (v. 10).

WORDS FROM WESLEY

2 Corinthians 12:9

My grace is sufficient for thee—How tender a repulse! We see there may be grace where there is the quickest sense of pain. My strength is more illustriously displayed by the weakness of the instrument. Therefore I will glory in my weaknesses, rather than my revelations, that the strength of Christ may rest upon me. The Greek word properly means, may cover me all over like a tent. We ought most willingly to accept whatever tends to this end, however contrary to flesh and blood. (ENNT)

DISCUSSION

It has been said that a person all wrapped up in him- or herself makes a very small package. That kind of person is bound to be a boaster no one likes to listen to. Discuss if all boasting is wrong.

1. Read 2 Corinthians 11:30–31. Why was Paul's boasting different from other kinds of boasting?

2. How do you know Paul's boasting wasn't egotistical?

3. Read 2 Corinthians 12:1–5. Why do you agree or disagree that Paul described his own experiences in these verses?

4. How would you describe "paradise" (v. 4)? Why are you longing for heaven?

5. Read 2 Corinthians 12:7–9. Why do you agree or disagree that Paul's thorn in the flesh was some kind of physical injury or illness?

6. Why doesn't God always answer the requests of a godly person?

7. How has a physical injury or illness drawn you closer to God?

8. How can Paul's testimony in verses 9–10 encourage a believer who is experiencing chronic illness?

PRAYER

Lord, we praise You as the God of our strength. Where we are weak, help us become strong in You. Thank You.

WORDS FROM WESLEY WORKS CITED

ENNT: *Explanatory Notes upon the New Testament,* by John Wesley, M.A. Fourth American Edition. New York: J. Soule and T. Mason, for the Methodist Episcopal Church in the United States, 1818.

PW: *The Poetical Works of John and Charles Wesley.* Edited by D. D. G. Osborn. 13 vols. London: Wesleyan-Methodist Conference Office, 1868.

WJW: *The Works of John Wesley.* Third Edition, Complete and Unabridged. 14 vols. London: Wesleyan Methodist Book Room, 1872.

OTHER BOOKS IN THE
WESLEY BIBLE STUDIES SERIES

Genesis (available February 2015)
Exodus (available April 2015)
Leviticus through Deuteronomy (available June 2015)
Joshua through Ruth (available June 2015)
1 Samuel through 2 Chronicles (available February 2015)
Ezra through Esther (available April 2015)
Job through Song of Songs (available February 2015)
Isaiah (available April 2015)
Jeremiah through Daniel (available February 2015)
Hosea through Malachi (available June 2015)
Matthew
Mark
Luke
John
Acts
Romans
1–2 Corinthians
Galatians through Colossians and Philemon
1–2 Thessalonians
1 Timothy through Titus
Hebrews
James
1–2 Peter and Jude
1–3 John
Revelation

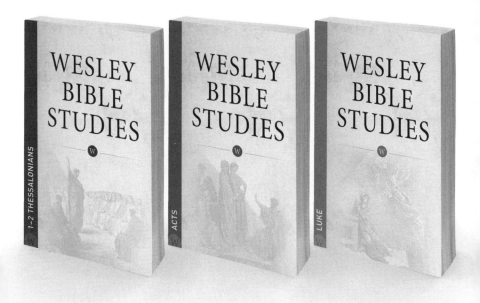